25 East 31st Street - N.Y

Katherine Winthrop Kean

To Mrs Kean
with all good wishes
[signature]

February 21st 1935 - California -

WHAT OF TOMORROW?

THE MACMILLAN COMPANY
NEW YORK · BOSTON · CHICAGO · DALLAS
ATLANTA · SAN FRANCISCO

MACMILLAN & CO., Limited
LONDON · BOMBAY · CALCUTTA
MELBOURNE

THE MACMILLAN COMPANY
OF CANADA, Limited
TORONTO

WHAT OF TOMORROW?

BY

OGDEN L. MILLS

NEW YORK
THE MACMILLAN COMPANY
1935

SET UP BY BROWN BROTHERS LINOTYPERS
PRINTED IN THE UNITED STATES OF AMERICA
BY THE FERRIS PRINTING COMPANY

CONTENTS

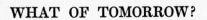

WHAT OF TOMORROW?

CHAPTER I

"WHAT OF TOMORROW?"

ANY American, who has faith in the political and economic principles that guided our nation throughout a century and a half of amazing progress, must be deeply concerned over the events of the last two years. We have witnessed the initiation and development of policies that in their ultimate implications must mean revolutionary changes in our governmental and economic structures.

Our form of government is a constitutional representative democracy, under which the chief emphasis is laid upon the inalienable rights and liberties of the individual citizen.

Our economic system is one of economic liberalism, which derives its motivating impulses from the creative energies of countless individuals, actuated by normal human aspirations and ambitions, and exercising wide freedom of choice; and which, though regulated by government, relies in the main on the automatic adjustments of a free economy.

For a democratic government of limited powers, careful of the rights of the States and of the liberties of the individual citizen, enforcing order and justice and maintaining equality of opportunity among a free and self-reliant people, there is gradually being substituted

1

in fact, and in the public mind, the conception of an all-powerful central government to which all men must look for security, guidance and assistance, and which, in turn, undertakes to control and direct the lives and destinies of all.

In the economic field, economic liberalism is being gradually supplanted by a centrally planned and controlled economy, which calls for constant intervention and direction by the State.

The two movements are the complementary halves of a single governmental philosophy which finds its supreme expression in the Fascist Government of Italy and the Nazi Government of Germany.

They are the very antithesis of everything America has stood for.

In the papers published in this volume, which were delivered as speeches in the course of the last twelve months, I have undertaken to analyze the character of the policies to which we are being committed in the name of recovery and reform, and their ultimate implications. I have endeavored to point out that they are neither novel nor progressive, but a reversion to prototypes tried throughout history, and with a uniform record of failure. I have tried to make clear that their initial application to our economic system, to which they are totally foreign, has served but to cripple its energies and to delay a recovery that is definitely within reach. And, above all, I have maintained that the basic assumption advanced in their justification, that our American institutions are a failure, is contradicted by our entire history.

To ascribe the present world depression,—which is directly related to the cataclysm of a world war for which we were in no wise responsible,—to the failure of our American governmental and economic systems, is a plain distortion of the facts.

There is a third and imminent danger to which two or three of these papers direct attention: Political control of the volume of money and credit and an inconvertible currency, on the one hand, and uncontrolled expenditures and continuing and growing deficits, on the other, lead inevitably to the disaster of uncontrolled inflation.

These articles were written, and this book is being published, because of my belief that those of us who have labored in the public service, and who hold sincere convictions on these great questions, owe it to those we have served in the past not to remain silent, no matter how inaudible our voice may be.

Holding the views I do, the opinions expressed could not be other than critical. But I have conscientiously endeavored to supplement specific criticisms with alternative suggestions of an affirmative character.

More particularly, I have outlined a program which, in my judgment, would do much to promote an early recovery; and throughout all the papers there runs the thread of a consistent political and economic philosophy:

Admitting that popular government will at times prove faulty, and popular passions on occasions lead to grievous injustice, in the long run I am confident that the many will show greater wisdom, unselfishness and fairness than a government of the one or of the few, however selected. For this reason, I place my faith in democracy, cumbersome though it may be, rather than in the swifter processes of autocracy or dictatorship, and in American Constitutional Government rather than in that modern adaptation of absolutism—the Fascist State.

I hold that government compulsion can never be an adequate substitute for individual initiative and effort; and that the creative energies of the individual and individual liberty must be safeguarded at all cost both from the tyranny of the few and of the many.

I prefer the collective judgment of the market-place to the assumed omniscience of the council chamber; the automatic adjustments of a free economy to the capricious and dogmatic decisions of bureaucracy; and the stimulating influences of the competitive process to the dead uniformity of government planning and control.

Government must determine general policies, must fix the rules and enforce them impartially, but I want it neither as a participant in the game nor as a dominant partner.

I am convinced that abuses may be corrected, the greater security which our people long for attained, and the progress to which they are accustomed maintained more surely within the framework of American institutions, and in accordance with their spirit and intent, than through their destruction or negation.

I believe that political, rather than economic, factors are delaying recovery, here and elsewhere; that nations need to cooperate more not less; that the barriers that at present dam up the flow of international trade must be removed; that order must replace confusion, certainty, doubt; to the end that the creative energies of millions throughout the world may be released, who need but wise and steadfast leadership and a sense of direction, to furnish the impulse that will restore well-being to human society.

CHAPTER II

WHERE DO WE GO FROM HERE?

THESE are stirring times. Great issues are gradually taking shape which will divide men as deeply and as uncompromisingly as any of the great issues of the past. In their decision the Republican Party has an immense responsibility, for surely the Party which during well-nigh three-quarters of a century, for all but seventeen years, has governed this nation has the vigor and constructive ability to develop a program based on time-tested principles to meet the new conditions of the day.

OPEN DISCUSSION AND POPULAR GOVERNMENT

As the minority and opposition Party, not now responsible for the conduct of the Government, our immediate function is to see that all important policies are subjected to such scrutiny, discussion and consideration as will permit the people to form a just appreciation of their wisdom and desirability. Open discussion and honest criticism are essential to the functioning of democratic institutions. In our country up to the present time, this commonplace saying has been taken for granted. Lately, however, it has assumed a new and all-important meaning. First, be-

6

cause, as we shall shortly see, free discussion and an informed public opinion are incompatible with the planned and managed national life which seems to be the ultimate objective of the present Administration; and, secondly, because it is apparent that even now there is a willingness to adopt the most sweeping measures, without that consideration which would permit the forming and expression of public opinion, and an obvious impatience with any criticism. We are witnessing revolutionary changes in our governmental and economic structures without popular mandate. We are being presented with a series of accomplished acts, the consequences of which in the future life of the nation are incalculable, and, in the name of national solidarity in time of stress, the voice of the people is afforded no opportunity to become audible.

Under these circumstances, silence is not a virtue, and, while mere partisan obstruction would be intolerable, it is the duty of the minority to insist that important measures shall not be adopted until they have been subjected to the tests of critical analysis and open discussion, unhampered by intimidation of any kind, to the end that public opinion may be informed and the people themselves afforded the opportunity to reach a sound judgment.

SUSPENSION OF CONSTITUTION

Popular government means faithful performance of the public will. The public will finds temporary expression in legislative and executive acts intended to deal with immediate problems, but the permanent will of the American people is embodied in the Constitution. They, and they alone, can change it. Until amended—and we have recently seen how promptly it can be amended in response to popular demand—any infraction or suspension of the fundamental law is a challenge to popular sovereignty. In all of its long history, no provision has ever been made for the suspension of the Constitution in time of emergency. This must unquestionably be due to the recognition that one of its most precious values is that it stands as a safeguard of our rights and liberties in times of stress.

If, then, the Congress and the President, by a mere declaration of an emergency, can in effect suspend the limitations of the fundamental law, it must be apparent that constitutional government as understood throughout our history ceases to exist, and that the Federal Government may be transformed over-night from a government of limited powers to one of unlimited authority over the life of every individual citizen.

GOVERNMENT BY MEN WITHOUT LIMITATIONS OF LAW

Not only have we witnessed what I believe is an unconstitutional attempt to extend the powers of the Federal Government beyond the limits contemplated by the basic law, but the exercise of the enormously expanded authority has been vested in the hands of a single individual. So that the citizen is deprived not only of the protection of the fundamental law but is subjected to arbitrary Executive action freed from the restrictions of legislative control. The abdication by the Congress and the delegation of powers to the Executive are in effect creating a government of men without any practical limitations of law.

The effect of the monetary legislation authorizing the President to issue $3,000,000,000 of greenbacks, to debase the gold content of the dollar, to fix the weight of the silver dollar and to provide for the free and unlimited coinage of silver, gave one man the right to alter as he sees fit the national monetary unit of value, and so directly to affect the economic situation of every family and individual in the land, altering the purchasing power of salaries and wages, the value of the products of farm, factory and mine, and of the investments, savings and insurance policies of all. We have to turn back many centuries to the days of absolute autocrats to find so great a power over the lives of millions of men lodged in the hands of a single fallible human being.

It is daily becoming more apparent that through the system of codes, the Federal Executive is attempting to establish detailed bureaucratic control over all business and industry, large and small, and over the economic activities of the individual citizen. It is true that in the first instance all American industries are invited to form their own codes; but they have no value unless approved by the President, and when approved they apply with the force of law even to those who have refused to sign. Moreover, the President may change the code at any time after it has been adopted, any violation of a code by any individual is made a crime, and the right of the President to refuse a license vests in him the power to destroy, even without resort to the vicious policy of boycott, the business of any man who refuses to comply with the arbitrary rules laid down by the central government.

INDIVIDUAL LIBERTY AND A PLANNED ECONOMY

When you sweep aside the glittering tinsel, the fact is that the Federal Government is today in effect telling the mechanic in California how many hours he may work, and what he may earn, the producer in Texas at what price he may sell his product, the manufacturer in New England what additions and improvements he may make to his factory, and the storekeeper in Kansas on what basis he may conduct his business. If the planners have their way, how long will it be before each farmer has to take out a license before cultivating his own farm and be compelled to operate under the regulation and supervision of Federal inspectors? These actions definitely violate the letter and spirit of the Constitution. They abolish the sovereignties of the States. They make of a government of limited powers one of unlimited authority over the lives of us all. They destroy America's greatest contribution to the cause of human freedom—the guarantee of individual rights against the arbitrary power of the government.

This Government was founded on the principle that the individual has the inalienable right to life, liberty and the pursuit of happiness. "Inalienable" means that these cannot be taken from him by the power of government. Liberty as we have understood it in this country has been the liberty of the individual to pursue the common callings of mankind, whether in farm, factory, mine or mercantile establishment, as he saw fit, so long as he didn't transgress the rights of others; and the police power vested in the State has been, and is, adequate to prevent transgression.

But if the Federal Government, acting through a centralized bureaucracy, may reach out to the farthest corners of this immense land, and regulate the daily life and occupations of the individual, liberty as we have understood it is dead, and a nation of free men will have become an aggregation of regimented subjects.

The whole conception of a planned and directed national economy is destructive of the most fundamental principles upon which the American system rests. It cannot be carried out unless the central government be vested with complete and arbitrary authority over the actions of individuals and the right to regiment them.

Mr. Walter Lippmann, one of the Administration's ablest supporters but not an advocate of a planned economy, in a most illuminating article has pictured the conditions essential to successful planning. He says: "Nobody honestly believes that planning can be carried out consistently among free men, that is to say, among men who have their own plans for their own lives; or that planning, in the full sense of the term, is possible where discussion is free; or that a social order can be managed if those who compose it are not regimented. In a planned society, no liberty is tolerable, which would delay or hinder the Executive. To manage a whole social order according to a central plan, human behavior must be predictable. The planner must know what men will produce and what they will consume; the only way to make sure of knowing this is to regiment men as producers and to ration them as consumers. For you can confidently predict how men will behave only when you have power to order their behavior. Thus a completely planned economy calls for an authoritarian state."

There is the unvarnished truth. In this Utopia to which the President is leading us, neither free discussion nor liberty will be tolerable, men will no longer be free in the sense that they may plan their own lives, but are to be regimented, directed and ruled by an all-powerful State.

Our ancestors gave their lives to make the individual the master of his own destiny, and the State the servant rather than the master of the people. The unexampled growth, progress and well-being of our people over a period of 150 years, and the wealth, resources, organization, standard of living and civilization of this, today, the most powerful nation on earth, testify to the soundness of their principles and to the wisdom and foresight with which they built.

Are we to destroy this inheritance, and to tear up the charter of our liberties in the vain hope that a small group of men, selected through political processes, may direct with greater sureness and foresight the life of the Nation than the people themselves? Where is the creative impulse, which originates only in

the individual, to come from? Granted the highest
wisdom in the selection of these directors, where are
they to find the necessary wisdom, knowledge, experience and vision? The truth is that there exists in the
world today no man or group of men who can visualize,
much less direct, the countless small streams that unite
to form the mighty river of American economic life.

The emergency measures are accomplished facts.
Whether we approve or not, there is little than can be
done. But if the effort is made, as it will be, to make
a regimented economy a permanent feature of our
national life, our Party should resist to the utmost.
We are not ready to admit that, with the spread of
knowledge, the rapid dissemination of information,
and the character and intellectual vigor of our people,
they are unable to govern themselves so as to cope
successfully with the new conditions of the day, but
must submit to the rôle of the governed.

THE N. R. A.

I would not have you infer that I am opposed to the
National Recovery Act and all its works. I am not. I
am opposed only to its extension far beyond what I
believe its original conception was, or, at least, ought
to have been. The idea that where industries are
genuinely national in scope, they might, through trade
associations, adopt, subject to the approval by the
Federal Government, regulations for their own guidance, intended to eliminate unfair and unsound practices and to promote progress and sound development,
has much to commend it. But this is something very

different from the wholesale attempt to reorganize business and industry of the country by substituting detailed bureaucratic control in the place of regulated individual control. It is perfectly possible to preserve a free economic system based on the maintenance of competition, and at the same time provide that business and industry may check abuses and promote progress through the formulation of policies for their own guidance, subject to government regulation based upon law. Surely, some way can be found of harmonizing the self-expression and liberty of the individual with the welfare of all.

RECOVERY THROUGH SPENDING

Turning, now, to the economic phases of the Administration's program, two clean-cut conceptions stand out: That the increase of consumer purchasing power through an enormous distribution of funds, and an increase in prices brought about by monetary manipulation, are the keystones to recovery. By spreading work and increasing the hourly rate of compensation, the N. R. A. contemplates putting more money into the hands of a great number of individual consumers, while through the Agricultural Adjustment Act, Public Works Administration and the Civil Works Administration, the Federal Government will distribute monthly many hundred million. In the meantime, monetary manipulation is relied on to force prices up.

These immense sums cannot be derived from national income. They must, therefore, be borrowed by making free use of the national credit. This means that as a nation, for the time being, we are no longer self-supporting. Just like the individual living on borrowed money, we are mortgaging our future. It is an uneconomic process, but, while it continues, it produces an appearance of business prosperity, stimulating as it does an increased demand for goods; and with basic forces the world over working toward recovery, it may help lead to a resumption of normal economic activities.

It is, however, perfectly clear that the process cannot be continued indefinitely. There is a limit to the national credit, and we cannot, short of inviting disaster, borrow up to the very point of exhaustion. At some stage or stages, therefore, a transition must be effected, and the nation once more become self-supporting. We must get back to the position where we can say with President Cleveland that "it is not the business of the Government to support the people; it is the business of the people to support the Government."

Again, it is idle to debate the wisdom or lack of wisdom of this attempt to spend our way out of the depression. We are definitely committed to this course, and we must now devote our best thoughts and efforts to make the venture successful.

The problem resolves itself into a race between business recovery and the exhaustion of the national credit. It follows that all unnecessary drains on the Federal Treasury should be avoided, and that all avoidable obstacles to recovery should be eliminated.

There is one aspect of the situation that cannot fail to make us thoughtful. Let me quote the statement of

a highly intelligent observer that has recently come
to my attention:

"For the first time in history a great nation has volun-
teered to assume the economic burdens of all its citizens.

"It says to its people that if you have become tired in
this long depression, and find your load too heavy, bring it
to us and we will take care of it and of you. If you are a
home owner and cannot meet your mortgage payments we
will take over the debt on easy terms. If you are a farmer
in danger of losing your place we will assume the mortgage.
If your crops have been selling at too low a price we will
pay you to raise smaller crops. If you are a business man
and weary with trying to meet competition we will regulate
that competition so it will not burden you. If you are a
railroad we will lend you money to meet your bond maturities. If you are a bank we will supply you with capital. If
you are an individual out of work we will give you a job.
If you are heavily in debt we will alter your money so as
to make that debt easy to pay.

"No such offers as these have ever before been made by
a responsible government. Many times in past history
similarly sweeping assurances have been put forward by
religious leaders seeking converts, but their promises have
concerned the future life instead of this one. These present
offers are immediate and tangible, and they are substantial
in convincingly real dollars. The administration is not only
presenting offers and giving assurances, it is making good
on its promises. While it continues to do so it will receive
the support of the millions who are the direct beneficiaries
of its philanthrophy. Public faith is being bought with
public works."

If that is a reasonably accurate picture—and it
seems to me that it is—are we not in danger of creating
a whole series of vested interests that cannot be sub-

sidized indefinitely from the public purse, and yet may politically become so powerful as to make it difficult for public officers to resist their demands? Here, again the time element is all-important, for the longer the citizen looks to the government for help, the more reluctant he becomes to resume once more the habit of self-reliance.

The dangers are there, and are unavoidable. They can, however, be minimized by scrutinizing every expenditure, by limiting them to what is strictly necessary to carrying out the program, by emphasizing at all times its emergency character, and by coordinating all efforts and sparing none to reach the real objective— the resumption of normal economic activity within the limit of time available.

The minority has here a real duty to perform. It must steadfastly resist any tendency to weakness on the part of the Government. It must oppose public squandering. It must constantly remind the Administration and the public of the true objective. It must relentlessly press the Administration to remove existing obstacles to recovery.

RISING PRICES AND FALLING PRODUCTION

The Administration's apparent faith in the value of a rise in prices *per se,* even if brought about by artificial means, such as monetary manipulation, may well constitute one of these obstacles. While a rise in prices may in some cases help debtors, and a rise in prices of agricultural commodities is essential in the interest of a better balanced price structure, a general rise in prices which tends to restrict industrial production is clearly undesirable and opposed to the goal sought to be attained by other means.

From this standpoint, certain features of the N. R. A. are definite obstacles to recovery. Under a normal process of recovery, we would have expected to witness first increased production, distribution and employment, followed by the reappearance of profits, an expansion of short-term credit, the rebirth of a capital market and of capital expenditures and a gradual rise in prices, costs and wages. The essential features of this process are that increased volume of production and employment are attained before the increase in wages, costs and prices takes place. Under the N. R. A., wages, costs and prices rise first, and increased volume of production is expected to follow. Unless the increased production does come, failure is inevitable, and to date the evidence indicates that the National Recovery Act itself has failed to stimulate greater volume. For instance, one of the conclusions reached by the National Industrial Conference Board as a result of a survey of New England industries conducted in conjunction with the New England Council was that "the consensus of opinion is that increased labor costs have increased sales prices, diminished production and increased inventory."

Again, there is no reason why the Public Works Administration and the Civil Works Administration, whose primary duty is to take care of the unemployed, should pay wages so high as to give serious competition to private industry, or so stimulate the prices of materials as to discourage private construction. After all, we cannot afford to create a situation where it will be impossible gradually to transfer men from the government emergency payroll to normal private payrolls.

Whether expenditures of the Federal government, running over half a billion a month, so distributed as in the first instance to increase consumer purchasing power, will be sufficient to overcome the handicap of increased costs and prices and uncertainty, and result in an increased production of goods, is all-important. But it is not the whole story.

THE HEAVY INDUSTRIES

These efforts are directed almost exclusively to stimulating the production of consumption goods. Assuming that they are successful, the further question arises as to whether the movement will in time spread to the production of durable goods. This is perhaps the crux of the problem of recovery. The so-called heavy industries today and throughout the depression have been the weak spot in our economic system. Until they recover, general recovery appears to be impossible.

How important they are in our national economy has been strongly brought out by Mr. Leonard Ayres, in a book recently published. He points out that, whereas in 1929 we produced consumption goods valued at about $30,000,000,000, the value of durable goods produced reached the colossal total of $40,-000,000; that throughout the depression the production of consumption goods was relatively stable, while the production of durable goods suffered a fearful collapse; and that even today the overwhelming majority of the unemployed in industry is composed of those who earn their livelihood in the production of so-called durable goods.

THE CAPITAL MARKET

While, from the standpoint of the Federal budget, the amount to be devoted to public works is large, these expenditures contrasted with the sums normally expended by the nation in the way of capital improvements of all kinds are not. Here, again, while government expenditures may in the first instance prime the engine, unless they are followed by a genuine flow of private capital into permanent improvements of all kinds, general recovery may be indefinitely delayed. After four years of the most severe restrictions, there is every reason to believe that a genuine need exists for all manner of capital expenditures, including replacements, improvements and new construction. Nor can there be much doubt that, given favorable conditions, an ample supply of long-term credit would be available.

OUR UNCERTAIN DOLLAR

The government would enormously enhance the prospect of an early recovery if it would remove the uncertainties that at present deter the business man from making long-term commitments and the investor from tying up his funds in long-time obligations. The chief of these are the uncertainty as to the govern-

response to the demands of business and commerce, but to meet current government expenditures, it would mean inflation of the crudest kind, disguised by a thin coating of gilt and silver.

But this is not the whole story. One of the most admirable features of our Federal Reserve System, the establishment of which constitutes one of the great constructive achievements of the Wilson Administration, was the provision for an elastic currency, expanding and contracting in accordance with the business and commercial needs of the country, as contrasted with the rigid and inelastic monetary system of the past; and the placing of the control of the volume of money and credit in the hands of central banks operated under government supervision, but free from political control. The program outlined in the President's Message clearly contemplates the impairment of these two central features of a sound monetary system. For an elastic currency, he would substitute a redundant and inelastic currency. For the non-political control of the central banks, he would substitute the political control of the Treasury.

Such a prospect is hardly reassuring.

AGRICULTURE

Finally we come to the problem of agriculture. Certain salient facts must be recognized to understand the nature of the problem. The difficulties are unquestionably due to an increase in production, a restriction of importing markets, and a gradual accumulation of stocks.

For instance, the world wheat supply (except of

Russia) increased from a pre-war average of about 3,000,000,000 bushels to an average of 3,600,000,000 bushels during 1926-30. During the period 1921-25, the average yearly production of the four chief exporting countries increased by 361,000,000 bushels, and even after European production came back to something like normal, these countries increased their production by an additional 220,000,000 bushels during the 1926-30 period. In the United States, production increased from a pre-war average of about 690,000,-000 bushels to over 880,000,000 during the period 1928-31.

In the meanwhile, first as a result of a return to more normal conditions, and later because of nationalistic tendencies, the markets of importing countries were being steadily narrowed by all manner of restrictions. Grains and animal products were particularly hard hit.

If we exclude cotton (exports of which were at the pre-war level), the volume of agricultural exports from this country in 1932-33 were but 64 per cent of the pre-war volume. In 1932 we exported only 32,000,000 bushels of wheat as compared with an average of 110,000,000 during the 1909-13 period, and 190,000,000 average during 1921-25.

Wheat imports of France, Germany and Italy fell from 232,000,00 bushels in 1928-29 to 47,000,000 in 1932-33.

Exports of pork have fallen from an average of 399,000,000 pounds in the period 1910-14 to 111,000,000 in 1932-33, while exports of lard have fallen from an average of 722,000,000 pounds in the years 1926-30 to 560,000,000 in 1932-33.

Our exports of tobacco to Europe have fallen from 347,000,000 pounds in 1924-25 to 224,000,000 in 1930-31.

If these products, including fruit and cotton, of which we produce substantial surpluses over and above our own needs, are dammed up in our own markets, prices fall, farmers are driven to the more intensive production of those products wholly consumed at home, and the price of these in turn is driven below the point of profitable production. Today, with the exception of cotton, all of our agricultural export products are suffering severely from foreign restrictions.

The facts speak for themselves. It is clear that we must produce less and we must sell more.

I am not inclined, therefore, to be too critical of the Administration's program, as strictly emergency measures. Conditions may well have justified both bonus payments and the debt relief program. But, looking to the future, I have no confidence that a premium payment will reduce production, and I am sure that a billion dollar processing tax will curtail consumption. Even today the government reports indicate that the reduction in winter wheat acreage is disappointing. On the other hand, the production of flour for domestic consumption during the four months July to November showed a falling-off of over 11 per cent.

Nor am I ready to accept the intolerable hardships involved in adjusting agricultural production to the needs of the domestic market. A practically completely self-contained and controlled national economy can doubtless be attained, but only at a frightful social cost, and by the enforced migration of millions of people from their homes and an all-round lowering of the standard of living.

I prefer to turn my attention to the possibilities, among others, of recovering lost markets and to the stimulation of increased consumption not only through the restoration of purchasing power at home but through the promotion of a greater prosperity and a higher standard of living the world over.

Granted that the difficulties are enormous, and that much time and patience will be required, this is even more true of the self-containment program. We will have to abandon the present policy of isolation and intense nationalism and to some extent modify recent tariff practices. This may sound strange coming from an orthodox Republican, but I have never understood that a sound system of protection, based on the difference of the cost of production at home and abroad, if intelligently applied, means the erection of impassable tariff barriers, the destruction of our commerce with the rest of the world, and the sacrifice of the efficient farmer to save the inefficient manufacturer.

I am prepared to take my stand with a great Republican President, President McKinley, who, in his last speech, delivered in Buffalo just before his assassination, said: "A system which provides a mutual exchange of commodities is manifestly essential to the continued and healthful growth of our export trade. We must not repose in the fancied security that we can forever sell everything and buy little or nothing."

A POLITICAL CREED

In conclusion, let me summarize this altogether too long a speech by stating some articles of a brief political creed:

I believe in a free press, open discussion and honest criticism as essential elements in the preservation of democratic institutions.

I am opposed to revolutionary change without popular mandate; and to government by men without any practical limitations of law.

I believe in our Federal form of government, with its system of State and local responsibilities, as contrasted with a centralized bureaucracy, and the powers, rights and duties of the Congress, as opposed to Executive dictatorship.

I am opposed to the attempt to reorganize the business and industry of the country by substituting detailed bureaucratic control in the place of regulated individual control.

I believe in an economic system based on individual freedom, and the maintenance of competition, under legal provision by which business and industry may check abuses and promote progress through the formulation of policies for their own guidance, subject to government regulation based upon law.

I believe that an unassailable national credit and a sound and stable currency are indispensable foundations of national prosperity.

I believe in the future the hardships of unemployment must be mitigated by the development of a sound system or systems of insurance.

I believe that the present destructive world economic war should be brought to an end by cooperation with other nations, looking to the stabilization of currencies, the establishment of a common medium of exchange, and the promotion of commerce and trade through the reopening of markets that are essential to the welfare of our agricultural industry.

If, in the formulation of national policies, these principles are steadfastly adhered to, I can maintain with undiminished strength my faith in the promise of American life.

January, 1934.

CHAPTER III

DICTATORSHIP OR DEMOCRACY

ONE hundred and forty-seven years ago as the authors were affixing their signatures to a document which William Gladstone described as "the greatest piece of work ever struck off at a given time by the brain and purpose of man," and which William Pitt prophesied would "be the wonder and admiration of all future generations," the venerable Benjamin Franklin, then eighty-one years old, looking toward the President's chair, at the back of which a rising sun was painted, observed:

"I have often and often, in the course of the session, and in the vicissitudes of my hopes and fears as to the issue, looked at that behind the President, without being able to tell whether it was rising or setting, but now at length, I have the happiness to know, that it is a rising and not a setting sun."

Dr. Franklin was right. The sun of American constitutional government was rising, heralding the dawn of a day that was to last well-nigh a century and a half and bring to a people worthy of its blessings greater progress, happiness, well-being and liberty than ever enjoyed by any people, any time, anywhere.

Today that sun appears to be setting over a nation

temporarily unmindful of its ancient virtues and apparently willing to follow a leadership that worships new and alien gods, and stands ready to substitute the sovereignty of the state for that of the citizen, collectivism for individualism, bureaucracy for democracy.

During the last year and a half, while the forms remain, the soul and spirit of American institutions have grown dim. For a democratic government of limited powers, careful of the rights of the state and local governments and of the liberties of the individual citizens, enforcing order and justice and maintaining equality of opportunity among a self-reliant people, confident of their ability to solve their own problems, there has been gradually substituted, in fact and in the public mind, the conception of an all-powerful central agency to which all men must look for security, guidance and assistance and which in turn undertakes to control and direct the lives and destinies of all.

The departure from the social, economic and political philosophies that have ever guided the life of our nation has been supported in the name of National Economic Planning. This, though labelled progressive and new, is a reversion to the principles of the seventeenth and eighteenth centuries. In the field of economics, it means the end of economic liberalism, upon which our civilization has been built. In the field of government, it calls for an authoritarian government, of which a dictatorship is the supreme expression, and which is exemplified in the modern world by the Fascist Government of Italy, the Nazi Government of Germany, and the Communist Government of Russia.

It is the negation of the fundamental principles set forth in the Constitution and of the supreme objective for which it was established.

The first and foremost of these principles is that the individual is supreme; that man is endowed, not by government but by his Creator, with certain inalienable rights; that to preserve those rights governments are instituted and that these governments derive their powers only from the consent of the governed.

The words of the preamble to the Constitution are significant. It begins, "We the people of the United States * * * ." "We the people do ordain and establish this Constitution." It comes from them. It is not imposed from above by an all-powerful ruler or government. The Government it creates exists only by virtue of their action. It has no other powers or authority save those they specifically grant it. It can turn only to them for additional authority. It is their creation, their instrument, their servant.

In this written Constitution they have fashioned its form, outlined its functions, set bounds to its authority. They have here embodied their permanent will unalterable save by their consent, obtained in the manner provided for.

What was the supreme objective which these men thus sought to attain? "To secure the Blessings of Liberty to ourselves and to our posterity." How could it be otherwise? For centuries men had struggled, faced persecution, suffered death in their slow progress toward the ideal of freedom. Now these men had attained it, after a bitter and protracted struggle of their own. A new and brilliant prospect lay open to mankind if only hard-won Liberty could be made secure:

The Liberty of the individual to live his life in his own way, free from interference by government, so long as he does not transgress the rights of others; irrespective of conditions of birth, to develop his talents as he sees fit; to enjoy the just rewards of his own industry and ability; to own property and to apply it to such uses as he deems wisest; to make contracts that will be respected; to save with the knowledge that his government will not confiscate his savings, nor reduce their value, nor limit his use of them; to enjoy freedom of thought, freedom of worship, freedom of speech and freedom of press; to live under a government of laws, not subject to the caprice of rulers or of temporary majorities, to be, in short, the sovereign citizen of a free republic, master of his government and of his destiny.

Our ancestors undertook to secure this Liberty by adopting a charter of government, every part of which, Hamilton declared, was a Bill of Rights. They made the central government one of limited powers and reserved to the state governments, that are closer to the people, all of the powers not specifically granted the central government. They divided the government into three separate and independent departments—the Executive, the Legislative and the Judiciary. They vested all authority to make laws, and more particularly to impose taxes, in their representatives in Congress. They provided that the Constitution and the laws enacted thereunder should be interpreted and applied by an independent Judiciary. They enacted the Bill of Rights which specifically protected the citizen from tyranny, oppression and arbitrary action, and guaranteed an impartial trial.

They imposed these limitations on their government and its agents not simply to narrow the opportunities of the vicious and profligate, but to establish bounds beyond which even the virtuous, actuated by high motives, might not trespass. For all experience had taught these men, who were thorough students of history, that the world has quite as much to fear from the well-meaning and weak as from the wicked and strong, and that liberty can be destroyed just as effectively by gradual encroachment and erosion as by direct and violent action.

During the last year and a half under the guise of emergency legislation, practically all of these limitations have been broken down or ignored.

As a result, the Federal government is no longer one of limited powers, but has almost unlimited authority over the life of the individual citizens. Today the Federal government in effect tells the wage-earner what he may earn and how long he may work; the farmer what and how much he may produce on his own farm; the merchant at what price he may sell his goods; the manufacturer what addition he may make to his plant and how much he may produce; the well owner how much oil he may flow. It controls the flow of capital and savings. It has entered into business in competition with its citizens.

Nowhere in the Constitution are these immense powers even suggested. If anyone had even hinted that they were contained in the Constitution at the time of its adoption, nothing is more certain than that there would have been no Constitution.

State lines have been obliterated. Not only does the grandmaster of the revived guilds and monopolies, General Johnson, declare that the Blue Eagle knows no boundaries, but the states themselves have abjectly surrendered their sovereignty by enacting blanket laws making statutes of the United States and all regulations, codes, and edicts the law of the state.

All legislative power is vested by the Constitution in the Congress, and specifically the power to impose taxes, and to regulate the value of money.

The right to impose taxes in his discretion has been granted the Secretary of Agriculture. The authority to fix the value of money has been transferred to the President, a power so great over the lives of men it has never been enjoyed by any save complete despots. The Congress has passed law after law which did little more than express a pious wish leaving it to the President to fill in the blank spaces as he sees fit, a power which the President in turn delegates to his innumerable bureaus.

In introducing one of these measures, the ranking Democrat in charge frankly admitted: "This bill makes the President of the United States a dictator for the time being. It is a benign dictatorship."

The fundamental guarantee that no man may be deprived of "life, liberty or property without due process of law" is being broken down. Innumerable bureaus and commissions have been set up. They write their own regulations, which have the force of law. They interpret them. They sit as judges and juries in enforcing them. Every effort is made to exclude review by courts or impartial tribunals. Enforcement is sought by intimidation, threats and the vicious and un-American boycott.

A special committee of the American Bar Association reports that the judicial branch of the Federal government "is being rapidly and seriously undermined * * * that Federal administrative agencies exercising judicial, in combination with legislative and executive powers, are substituting a labyrinth in which the rights of individuals, while preserved in form, can easily be nullified in practice."

Thus, contrary to the spirit and intent of our institutions, subverting the limitations designed to protect them, an all-powerful centralized bureaucracy is being established; local self-government and responsibility are being undermined; and the liberty and rights of the citizen are no longer secure.

Is it any wonder that leading American statesmen, Democrats and Republicans alike, are warning the people to beware? Says Senator Borah: "Of all forms of government which have ever been permitted to torture the human family, the most burdensome, the most expensive, the most demoralizing, the most devastating to human happiness and the most destructive of human values is a bureaucracy. It has destroyed every civilization upon which it has fastened its lecherous grip."

And Mr. John W. Davis: "It is not necessary to

uproot or fell a tree in order to destroy it. It can be killed by the slower and equally fatal process of girdling the trunk. * * * Representative democracy is by universal acknowledgment a difficult form of government. * * * But the blood of patriots has watered it, the soil of freedom has fed it, and the liberties of men have found shelter in its shade. It would die, if die it must, a nobler death in the lightning and the storm than by the slow strangulation of an engirdling bureaucracy."

And Chief Justice Pattangall of the Maine Supreme Court: "when men are denied the right to buy and sell the products of their labor in the open market place, fixing the prices of the goods in which they deal by bargain with their fellows; when the farmer is forbidden to sow and reap on the land he owns according to his own best judgment; when every detail of the daily business life of the citizen is ordered by officials, not of his choosing; when written agreements cease to have a binding force, even upon government itself—the nation which the Civil War was fought to preserve will have ceased to be."

And former Secretary of State and Senator, Mr. Elihu Root, referring to these new powers assumed by government, makes this observation: "It is no party matter. It is not to be determined solely or chiefly by immediate effects. Our future social organization and the permanence of our national union may well be at stake, for the proposal appears to involve an abandonment of limitations on official power which, rightly or wrongly, we have considered essential to our free government."

We are sacrificing our birthright without even getting the mess of pottage. Planned Economy is not working in this country any more than it has ever worked anywhere. The clumsy hands of government—the right frequently not knowing what the left is doing—are halting the existing mechanism and throttling the normal forces that should be working for recovery. To move ahead there must be a sense of direction. This country is being reformed in every direction. It isn't moving in any. Nature has made a grim mockery of the agricultural policy. Industrial production is proceeding at a lower rate than a year ago, and not much about what it was in September, 1932. Instead of re-employment the number of those on the stupendous relief roll grows steadily day by day.

The amazing break with the past is sought to be justified on the grounds that our representative constitutional government, though suitable enough for the conditions of its day, does not meet those of our own; and that our system of economic liberalism has failed.

Let us examine these charges.

The Constitution was not established to satisfy the views and aspirations of a single generation, but to secure the blessings of enduring principles to all posterity. It is not the mere creation of spontaneous invention, or an ephemeral body from which all life would depart with the circumstances that gave it birth. Our Constitution has its roots deep in the remote past. It is based on the accumulated governmental experience of the race. It derives its strength and durability from principles that are as old as human nature and as immutable.

What is perhaps even more significant from the standpoint of immediate issues is that there is not a single one of these experiments that has not its counterpart in history and was not familiar to the authors of the Constitution—authoritarian governments, planned economies, controlled production, the fixing of prices, wages and hours of labor, the fostering of monopolies, the debasement of currencies, the repudiation of obligations, the whole New Deal in short. Already in 1787 the so-called New Deal was an old, old Deal, dealt from a pack thumbed by the fingers of countless kings, despots and tyrants all down the centuries. The framers knew it so well that they set up a system of government that would make these and other such futilities and follies difficult, if not impossible. And they did this job so thoroughly that when once more mankind sought to yield to its most persistent weakness—inability to profit from the experience of the past, it became necessary to subvert and overstep the boundaries and limitations which these wise and far-sighted men had set up.

The American system of individual liberty under democracy has not failed. It is the greatest success in all history. For centuries the world had stagnated under the burden of its authoritarian governments directing with heavy hand the lives of men. In the new world the creative power of the individual human spirit was suddenly freed. Under this dynamic impulse, we see a young and weak nation master a continent, grow into one of the mighty peoples of the earth and by whatever standard you care to measure, achieve a greater degree of progress in one century than all mankind in the preceding two thousand years.

Unlike previous forward movements, the mass of the people were the chief beneficiaries of this progress. They have enjoyed a greater and progressive diffusion of wealth, greater comfort, greater security, greater educational opportunities and a higher standard of living than average men and women at any time, anywhere. And these accomplishments are due not to the wisdom of princes and rulers, but to the virtues, character and energies of the people themselves, living under a system of government that brought unlimited opportunity to all men.

True, we were not successful in warding off a worldwide depression. It had its origin in the monstrous dislocations and demoralization of war. It has overwhelmed all nations. But by what process of reasoning are we justified in judging the merits of any system by a comparatively brief period of misfortune. There has been more of America than the past five years; there have been seven score years of it and it has been good.

True, perfection has not been attained; there is unlimited opportunity for further advance; there are weaknesses to be corrected; and under this as well as any other system individuals have failed us. But I challenge anyone to name any other form of government that has contributed more to the welfare of mankind and has yielded any such results. Furthermore, since it does not depend on the wisdom and virtue of a small group, however selected, but draws its strength and resources from the people themselves, as long as there is health in the nation it can constantly renew its vitality at the source and find there the recuperative forces with which to overcome all weaknesses.

The truth is that today, as at all times, there are men who conscientiously believe that the few, whether so-called intellectuals or aristocrats, are better able to plan and to direct the lives of the many than they themselves. They reject the whole conception of economic liberalism with its faith in the automatic adjustments of a free economy and in the progress to be achieved by the unfettered energies and ambitions of countless individuals exercising the widest freedom of choice. They believe as did the earlier economists of the mercantile school that the constant intervention of the state in the economic life of the nation is essential. And this economic belief inevitably compels them to insist on an authoritarian state.

This is the philosophy underlying the New Deal. It cannot be squared with the basic principles of our Constitution.

Whether we like it or not, we are called upon to choose between two irreconcilable philosophies of government. The conception of the sovereignty of the state and that of the sovereignty of the citizen cannot be reconciled any more than a planned economy can be with economic liberalism. Both are the implacable enemies of freedom.

Mussolini's declarations of "everything within the state, nothing without the state * * * ." "The state is resuming its rights and its prestige as the sole and supreme interpreter of the needs of society," and the proclamation in the Declaration of Independence that "all men are endowed by their Creator with certain inalienable rights" and that "governments derive their just powers only from the consent of the governed" are as far apart as the poles.

Between those two ideals America must choose once more as it already chose a century and a half ago.

With incalculable consequences to ourselves and to future generations, we shall make an irretrievable mistake if we assume they can be compromised; and if, in the desire for swifter action than the machinery of democracy can afford, if in the vain hope that greater wisdom will be found in public servants than in the people they serve, we tear down the limitations imposed on government and entrust it with supreme and irrevocable power over the lives of us all.

There is no middle ground between governing and being governed, between absolute sovereignty and liberty, between tyranny and freedom.

There can be no such thing as a Planned and Controlled Economy as long as men remain free—free to earn what they want and can, to spend their earnings as they see fit, or having saved, to invest their savings as they deem wisest, to acquire property and to put it to such productive use as they desire. For Government cannot plan and direct when it cannot foresee; and since it cannot foresee the actions of 120,000,000 people if each is allowed to proceed in his own unpredictable way, it must either forego planning or bring their actions under control.

It is equally true that a Planned Economy spells the death of representative democracy. Our form of government is beautifully adapted to perform its intended functions, limited as they are in character, to lay down and enforce definite rules of conduct and to determine broad lines of national policy. It is very ill adapted to the certainty, promptness and decision that are requisite in the conduct of business affairs.

How long do you think a single business would survive if it were run by two boards of directors, composed in the one case of four hundred and thirty-five members and in the other of ninety-six, representing on a geographical basis stockholders who not only owned the company but did business with it; with an independent executive vested with overriding authority; the decision of the Boards and the Executive subject to review by an independent group of nine other men? If such an organization is obviously incapable of running a single business, what reason is there to believe it can successfully direct all businesses, large and small, of every kind and variety?

Granted that they were planted in shallow soil, why in country after country in continental Europe have democratic institutions foundered, to be replaced by dictatorships? To me the explanation seems simple enough. Overwhelmed by the tragic consequences of the war, pressed on all sides by new and difficult problems, the people turned to their governments for salvation. These in turn found that complete responsibility demanded complete power; that decision called for concentration of that power; and that representative parliaments and the cumbersome machinery of democracy were incapable of assuming the multitudinous functions of economic direction. So we see these parliaments first delegating vast powers to the executive; then satisfied merely to record his wishes and finally, fading from the scene altogether.

We have witnessed something of the kind in our country. The delegation by the Congress to the President of what are in effect legislative powers was a silent admission that if the government of the United States is to assume the detailed conduct of the nation's business, such direction cannot be provided for by law but must largely be left to executive discretion.

The germ of destruction has already been planted. The contagion of ideas is already evident. The urge to shed our burdens by passing them on to government is already at work. But let us not forget that responsibility, self-reliance and liberty are inseparable. When "government assumes the guardianship of bewildered citizens," there can be no illusions as to how the story will end.

In a recent lecture, the distinguished Swedish economist, Professor Cassel, after expressing the gravest apprehension "at the actual drift of the revolution threatening our civilization," remarked:

"The leadership of the state in economic affairs which advocates of Planned Economy want to establish, is, as we have seen, necessarily connected with a bewildering mass of governmental interferences of a steadily cumulative nature. The arbitrariness, the mistakes and the inevitable contradictions of such policy will, as daily experience shows, only strengthen the demand for a more rational coordination of the different measures and, therefore, for unified leadership. *For this reason Planned Economy will always tend to develop into Dictatorship.*"

But, you may say, after all, free elections ensure ultimate control to the people. Be not deceived. How long can free elections remain free after government attains supreme power over the lives of men? How much real authority was exercised by the German people in the August plebiscite? Or by the French people in confirming the power assumed by their two Napoleons?

Finally, the public good is invoked as a justification, and the claim advanced that economic and property rights must be sacrificed in the interests of human rights. But what dictator or despot, ancient or modern, ever professed to act otherwise than in the public good? How long can human liberties survive the power to defend them? And what power remains after initiative, self-reliance, opportunity and economic independence are all gone?

May I once more refer you to this impartial witness who has had the opportunity to observe the process close at hand?

"Economic dictatorship is much more dangerous than people believe. Once authoritative control has been established it will not always be possible to limit

it to the economic domain. If we allow economic freedom and self-reliance to be destroyed, the powers
standing for Liberty will have lost so much in strength
that they will not be able to offer any effective resistance against a progressive extension of such destruction
to constitutional and public life generally. And if this
resistance is gradually given up—perhaps without
people ever realizing what is actually going on—such
fundamental values as personal liberty, freedom of
thought and speech and independence of science are
exposed to imminent danger. What stands to be lost is
nothing less than the whole of that civilization that
we have inherited from generations which once fought
hard to lay its foundations and even gave their life for
it."

Say what they will, I cannot believe that as a people
we no longer have the energy, the self-reliance and the
courage to run our government and to manage our own
affairs; that our business leaders as a class are so cor-
rupt that they can no longer be trusted; that in this
country success no longer represents merit and sacrifice, but unscrupulous adventure or survival under the
law of the jungle. But if all this be true and necessitate
an all-powerful government to guard and guide us, in
the name of common sense, how long will that government itself remain pure?

Yes, "America must choose." And when the Secretary of the Treasury, Mr. Morgenthau, speaking for
the Administration, declares that this government is
assuming the guardianship of a bewildered citizenry,
the old-fashioned American with his faith in a clear-

visioned, valiant, self-reliant people, cannot help but wonder how much time is left.

While the darkness of despotism is settling over most of the weary and perplexed peoples of the Old World, and while our own government, in the twilight of democracy, gropes and fumbles by the dim rays of mediæval doctrine, mankind awaits the answer of the American people, an answer once given in the bloody agony of fraternal strife, the answer to the question posed at Gettysburg by the rugged personification of all our virtues, the immortal Lincoln: "Whether a nation conceived in liberty can long endure, and whether government of the people, by the people and for the people is to perish from the earth."

September, 1934.

CHAPTER IV

ON OUR WAY—TO INFLATION

IT is time the country woke up to the fact that the road we are traveling leads directly to progressive and uncontrolled inflation.

Uncontrolled expenditures and increasing deficits, on the one hand, and authority to issue inconvertible currency and to manufacture credit, on the other, if unduly prolonged, sooner or later mean inflation just as certainly as one and one make two.

Prior to March 4, 1933, the Executive branch of the Government had no authority to issue currency on its own initiative, and the control of fundamental credit was vested in a non-political agency, the Federal Reserve System. The public has not yet grasped the full significance of the fact that today the Executive branch of the Federal Government possesses in full measure the authority to issue currency on its own initiative, and has at the same time secured control of the credit mechanism by political encroachment on the independence of the Federal Reserve System and by the extraordinary powers granted the Secretary of the Treasury.

Under the pressure of budgetary difficulties, political necessity and its own spending policies, how long will

47

it be before the Government yields to the temptation to use these immense powers to meet its financial needs by manufacturing either money or credit, or both? Inclination and opportunity are dangerous partners.

To understand the revolutionary change that has taken place, and all of its implications, it is necessary to examine the American monetary and credit system as it existed prior to the "Roosevelt Revolution."

At that time ours was a gold standard country, that is to say, all currency as a practical matter was redeemable on demand, in gold dollars, the gold content of which was fixed by law.

Whatever the weaknesses of the gold standard—and in my judgment they are fewer and less serious than those of any other system—it has three outstanding merits: It inspires confidence in the currency. It furnishes a definite link with other currencies, thus facilitating international dealings. It provides a nonpolitical mechanism of control over the total supply of money.

When I was Secretary of the Treasury, I had no authority to issue Treasury currency in my discretion.

This did not mean a rigid and inflexible currency and credit system, for our Federal Reserve Banks could expand and contract currency and credit in response to the legitimate needs of commerce and industry, subject, of course, to the limit imposed by the ultimate gold reserve—a gold reserve which ever since the establishment of the Federal Reserve System has been more than ample for our needs.

If revenues were not adequate to cover expenditures,

the Secretary of the Treasury could meet deficits only through the public offering of Government securities; and his ability to sell them at reasonable rates depended on jealous maintenance of the credit of the Government.

All this meant that the Executive Officers of the Government could operate only within the definite limits which prudence, long experience and the laws laid down by the Congress had established; while the control of credit was entrusted to a non-political body, the Federal Reserve System.

The subject is of sufficient importance to justify closer examination.

Aside from metallic money—that is, gold, silver dollars and subsidiary coins—our pre-1933 currency consisted of: gold certificates, which could be issued only against a full coverage of free gold; dollars and silver certificates, limited to $570,000,000; United States notes, limited to $346,000,000; national bank notes, backed by Government bonds and limited in amount by the paid-in capital of the issuing banks and by the amount of bonds bearing the circulation privilege; Federal Reserve Bank notes, issued to replace national bank notes; and Federal Reserve notes.

These last furnished the flexible element in our currency system. They were issued not by the Treasury but by the Federal Reserve Banks. They could be issued in any amount in response to credit and currency demands, save that they had to be backed by at least 40 per cent of their value in gold and the balance by commercial paper, or by the notes of borrowing member banks secured by government bonds.

This brief summary makes it entirely clear that neither the President nor the Secretary of the Treasury could issue currency in their discretion, or control the amount issued. The door to this means of financing deficits and thus starting inflation was locked and barred. The people and their representatives had evidently profited by the lessons of history.

Centralized management of the total supply of currency and credit was entrusted to the twelve Federal Reserve Banks, under the supervision of the Federal Reserve Board. Generally speaking, the total volume of credit and currency was determined by the current needs of trade and production. But through its rate of discount and its ability to put money in the Market or take it out by the purchase or sale of Government securities and commercial paper, the Federal Reserve System exercised a measure of control which could be made extremely effective if vigorously applied at the proper moment.

Thus, flexibility was secured, and, to the extent that management was desirable, it was afforded by the central banks and not by the political authorities.

To be sure, there has been talk of Treasury domination of the Federal Reserve System. But whatever may have been true of the War and post-War periods, in my twelve years in Washington, during six of which I was in a position to observe at close range, I know of no single instance where Federal Reserve policy was governed by Treasury needs.

I cannot emphasize too strongly the importance of non-political control of our monetary and credit systems.

Money and credit are the life-blood of our economic system. They should flow in response to the needs of the entire economic organism. To the extent that the flow needs to be regulated, this should be done by experts, concerned with the health of the economic body as a whole, and free from any selfish interests.

Government finance, while important, is not a dominating element. Yet it is all-important to those entrusted with its care. Their political fortunes are intimately connected with its successful management. They are but human when they confuse the cash needs of the Government with the credit needs of the country. And experience shows that in times of stress this is just what they do.

The picture today is a very different one. The Secretary of the Treasury has described the new monetary system as "the 1934 model gold bullion standard," "streamlined," "air flow," and with "knee action." At that, I'm not sure he did it full justice.

Our currency is an inconvertible paper currency. For all practical purposes, control over the amount of money is political in character. The President and the Secretary of the Treasury are in a position to pump it out almost as they see fit.

Gold certificates may be freely issued against gold held in the Treasury up to the legal value of such gold. Through the devaluation of the gold dollar and the seizure of all gold, the Treasury acquired a fund of

$2,800,000,000 of free gold. Under very slight limitations, this entire amount can be made into active money.

The President, at his discretion, may further devalue the dollar within certain limits, and thus increase the monetary gold and currency supply.

The President may provide for the unlimited coinage of silver with any fixed ratio to gold that he may determine.

Under the Silver Purchase Act, the President is directed to acquire silver until one-fourth of the value of the monetary stock is in silver. Under the terms of this law, silver certificates may be issued up to almost one billion eight hundred million dollars.

The President may direct the Secretary of the Treasury to issue up to $3,000,000,000 of United States notes or greenbacks.

The President may direct the Secretary of the Treasury to enter into an agreement with the Federal Reserve Banks to buy up to $3,000,000,000 of Government securities, thus putting that amount of primary credit or bank reserves into the market.

The President may further revalue the standard silver dollar, and thus presumably further increase the supply of silver currency.

The authority of the Federal Reserve System over the money market has been completely overshadowed by the immense powers granted the Secretary of the Treasury. He may deal in gold and silver at home and abroad in foreign exchange. He may deal in Government securities. Mr. Morgenthau possesses greater financial power than any individual has ever been permitted to exercise in this country.

Thus, complete control over the currency and credit supply of the country has been centralized in the hands of the political authorities at the very moment when, owing to immense and growing deficits, they are under the greatest temptation to misuse it. It is difficult to imagine a more unfortunate combination of circumstances.

It is high time to stand off from the picture, and take a good look at it, and particularly to compare it with the classic pattern of inflation.

Inflation almost always begins in budget troubles. With variations, it follows this course:

1. In the early days of an unbalanced budget, deficits may be financed through the sale of long-time securities to the public and investment institutions, though they are not necessarily so financed, as money market factors may predominate. So long as financing can be done in this way, at not unduly high rates, since maturities may be spread out, since the debt is widely held and since the deficit is financed from savings, the unbalanced budget is not as yet a matter of serious concern.

2. As deficits continue and the government shows no intention of putting its finances in order, the second stage is reached. The public shuns long-term issues. The government, if it wants to finance cheaply, is forced to resort to shorter loans. This is due to growing uncertainty and to the incipient fear that payment may be made in depreciated currency.

3. When the public loses interest even in the shorter maturities, the third stage is reached. Banks continue to buy. Banks can afford to go along for a very considerable period so long as they adhere to short-term paper, because, while they may be paid off at maturity in depreciated currency, they can also pay off their depositors in depreciated currency. This stage may be said to represent the beginning of credit inflation.

4. Finally, we come to the fourth stage. The banks feel that in justice to their depositors they cannot increase their investment in Government securities, and they hesitate to be a party to further inflation. When this stage is reached, the government is compelled to choose whether it will balance the budget by economies and higher taxes, or whether it will resort to forced inflation. Forced inflation may take the form of currency inflation or credit inflation. If it takes the form of direct currency inflation, the government simply starts the printing-press. If it takes the form of indirect currency inflation, the government sells its paper directly to the central bank or banks in exchange for currency or credit emitted by the latter. In this country it would simply sell its paper to the Federal Reserve Banks, taking in return a book credit, against which it could draw by check.

Where, judged by these tests, do we stand?

It is impossible to be dogmatic on this point, but it is probably fair to put it this way: While not completely out of the first stage we have entered the second, with the third in sight. Moreover, there is no question that many persons would like to see the government voluntarily enter the fourth stage, or that the government is actively considering what it will do if forced into that stage.

The budget has now been out of balance for five years. For the fiscal year 1934, the deficit, exclusive of debt retirement, amounted to $3,630,000,000. There can be no doubt that the present fiscal year will likewise witness a large excess of expenditures over receipts. Just how large, it is difficult to estimate at this time. Expenditures for the first quarter of this year amounted to $1,517,000,000, as compared with $923,-000,000 a year ago, and it is ominous that so-called emergency expenditures increased from $297,000,000 to $841,000,000, in spite of the fact that the Reconstruction Finance Corporation showed a credit balance of $141,000,000, as compared with a debit balance of $128,000,000 in 1933.

If the deficit for this fiscal year is approximately what it was last year, it is estimated that the Federal debt will amount to about $30,000,000,000, an increase of $14,000,000,000, or more than 87 per cent from the low point.

Not only has the debt been following the classic pattern, so far as size is concerned, but in its general character as well. Its composition has changed materially, as also has its distribution.

On December 31, 1930, when the total debt was $16,026,000,000, the short-term obligations—that is, the portion falling due within five years—amounted to but $3,661,000,000, or 23 per cent. On September 30 last, of the total debt of $27,190,000,000, no less than

$14,359,000,000 or 52.8 per cent, represented debt payable within five years.

When we turn to the distribution of the debt, we find that that, too, has been following the expected lines. Professor E. C. Harwood, Director of the American Institute of Economic Research, has recently reported that, whereas, at the end of 1930, $5,000,000,000 of the $16,000,000,000 public debt outstanding was held in the banking system—that is, slightly more than 31 per cent—by September of this year bank holdings represented $12,500,000,000 out of a total of $26,800,-000,000. That is, more than 46 per cent.

In other words, of the expansion of $10,800,000,000 in the public debt in this period, $7,500,000,000 or, roughly, 70 per cent, has found its way into the banks. Thus, we have the fundamental foundation for inflation—a chronically unbalanced budget, with the floating debt expanding at a rapid rate, and the drift of purchases strongly away from investors and into the banks.

But these figures, while ominous enough in themselves, do not begin to tell the whole story. Back of them loom considerations which make them even more dangerous.

The Administration has committed itself, either by deliberate promise or by implication, to two major policies that contain grave inflationary possibilities. One of these is the policy of reflating prices to an arbitrarily selected level, such as that prevailing in 1926; the other is the espousal of the Keynes notion that the way to produce business recovery is to spend billions upon billions of the public money in "priming the pump."

Far from evidencing any real desire to bring the budget into balance, the President has refused to commit himself to anything resembling a policy of stabilization or economy. While he has never clearly enunciated his monetary policies, he has let it be known that, contrary to the universal view of recognized monetary authorities, he does not regard the issuance of "non-interest-bearing notes" (greenbacks) to meet maturities or certain other items as currency inflation.

In spite of growing demand for relief and the undeniable fact that recovery is not yet in sight, relief needs alone—if only relief can be freed from waste and politics and divorced from the "prime the pump" spending theory—will not, in my judgment, occasion any such deficit or deficits as to cause a budgetary crisis.

The danger does not lie there. But rather in the Administration's faith in government spending as a means of promoting recovery, and in policies which, interfering as they do with normal economic processes, and thus retarding recovery, produce situations calling for more and more spending.

As I had occasion to point out recently, an artificial structure is being created which is largely dependent on government credit. When monetary manipulation, or the N. R. A., forces prices up faster than the increase in current purchasing power, the Federal Treasury must close the gap. When the farmer curtails production, his income must be supplemented by a government subsidy. When business, deprived of its normal

energies, shows signs of slowing down, it must be galvanized into artificial activity by a fresh outpouring of
funds.

A whole series of vested interests in government
spending are being created. Any attempt to slow down
the process or go into reverse must occasion temporary
losses, which will give rise to determined economic and
political resistance from many quarters.

I do not say the Administration cannot turn back;
but unless there is a very definite change in public sen-
timent, it has loosed forces that will drive us irresistibly
forward along the road we are now traveling; and at
the end of that road there's a precipice.

As the Government continues to spend much more
than its income, and as deficit is piled upon deficit,
with no end in sight, events will follow the course
already outlined.

Investors will show increasing reluctance to purchase
securities, poured out in constantly increasing amount.
In time, they will stop entirely.

The banks will continue to subscribe for a longer
period, particularly as they are in possession of enormous excess reserves. But, as excess reserves disappear,
and as budgetary difficulties grow greater, they will
feel it impossible to continue to finance the full needs
of the government.

Under our old system, as such a situation gradually
arose, the government would sooner or later have been
compelled to modify its policies. Increasing interest
rates and a narrowing market for government securities
would long since have warned the Secretary of the

Treasury, in unmistakable signals, of the danger ahead. If tax revenues were inadequate, and he could no longer borrow, only one course remained open—to put the Government's financial house in order,—in such a country as ours by no means an impossible task.

All the spenders and inflationists to the contrary notwithstanding, these definite checks were of inestimable benefit to the Government, and of even greater benefit to the country. Bankruptcy by the slower process of gradual depreciation of a country's currency and the gradual melting away of its savings, though it takes longer, is none the less bankruptcy, with all that it entails in the way of loss to the great mass of the people.

Under the old order, we were warned in time. Under the new, with the whole automatic safety-device mechanism gone, we may be led over the precipice blindfolded.

Today, as the ordinary and legitimate credit sources dry up, the government can, and almost inevitably will, turn to those which, all experience teaches, lead to disaster. It may finance itself in one of two ways: It may borrow directly from the Federal Reserve Banks, or it may begin to make use of its currency-issuing powers.

The methods are different, but the results are identical.

Let us have a look at the types of inflation possible under the new laws:

The first section of the Inflation Act of 1933 provides for the purchase by the Federal Reserve Banks of Government securities up to $3,000,000,000 in amount.

This was the favorite device employed in the various post-war inflations of Europe. In France, such operations were designated "Treasury advances." How insidious this type of inflation is may be gathered from what happened in the case of France. At the beginning of the War, the French Treasury and the Bank of France reached an accord whereby the Treasury might receive accommodations of this sort up to 2,900,000,000 francs, and the bank was authorized to issue notes up to 5,200,000,000 francs.

It was so easy and convenient to borrow this way, however, that, to quote from Robert Murray Haig, "the limit sprang lightly out of reach every time it was approached." Before the episode was over, the limit of "advances" had been moved up to 39,500,000,000 francs, and the limit of currency circulation had moved close to 60,000,000,000 francs. Even that limit, it was revealed in 1925, had been secretly exceeded as a result of collusion between the Bank of France and the Finance Minister.

Secondly, in addition to the "ways and means advances" that may be obtained from Federal Reserve Banks, the government has authority to issue $3,000,-000,000 of greenbacks, with which we have already had one sad experience.

And, in the third place, the government may issue other forms of paper currency no longer redeemable in gold.

When the government manufactures and uses Federal Reserve credit, or its own currency, to pay current bills, the funds so distributed automatically create a new artificial purchasing power, which exercises a direct and immediate influence on prices. But the movement does not stop here. It snowballs. The currency or credit flows into commercial banks. Each dollar of currency constitutes a bank reserve upon which a deposit credit of at least $10.00 may be created.

Thus, the $3,000,000,000 of Federal Reserve Bank credit would eventually find its way to the reserves of the commercial banks. The greenbacks would add an equal amount. $2,800,000,000 in gold profits might add an additional $2,800,000,000. We would have a total of $8,800,000,000 in member bank reserves, which might be made the basis of an expansion of member bank credit in excess of $88,000,000,000. And this leaves out of consideration the present excess reserves of $1,700,000,000, the more or less indeterminate addition that would result from the issuance of silver certificates and the effects of a return of currency from hoarding, that might be expected to come with inflation. Unrestrained credit and currency inflation could call into being upward of $125,000,000,000 in member bank credit.

What does $125,000,000,000 mean? What does $20,-000,000,000 mean? Dr. Benjamin Anderson tells us that the whole series of booms between 1922 and 1928 were financed by an expansion of less than $15,000,000,-000 in deposits. He tells us we financed the War on a bank credit expansion of less than $6,000,000,000.

When we consider, further, that the total deposits in commercial banks as of November first amounted to $32,500,000,000, that the total contraction of bank credit during the great deflation amounted to about $15,000,000,000, these potential bank credit expansion figures are literally staggering.

As Professor Young of the Wharton School of Commerce and Finance, referring to the new powers granted the Executive, says: "If all of these powers were to be applied jointly or in close succession, no competent authority would deny that they would involve a total increase in the currency supply of theoretically incalculable proportions. And there would be no serious doubt of an accompanying elevation of domestic prices, wholly defiant of any formal admonitions and gestures of control. * * * No one could predict to what heights prices would finally advance, how fast would be the tempo of the rise, or how aggravated the price and production dislocations would finally become, but it can safely be stated that the monetary forces for the rise would be so powerful, and rising prices would finally acquire so great a momentum, irrespective of price and trade derangements, that no subsequent governmental action would prove politically expedient or economically effective in bringing the inflationary upswing under rational control."

In other words, if the Administration makes full use of the powers it now possesses, the country will be engulfed by a major inflationary movement.

The crushing weight of the disaster will be borne by the entire nation, but those least able will bear the heaviest burden. The first impact will be borne by the endowments of great public welfare institutions, the savings deposits of the poor and the life insurance policies of the foresighted and thrifty. This is bad enough, but it's not the whole story. Referring to the French inflationary debauch at the end of the eighteenth century, Von Sybel has this to say: "By the end of 1795 the worthless paper money was almost exclusively in the hands of the working classes, employees, men of small means, whose property was not large enough to invest in stores of goods on nation lands. Financiers, although they suffered heavily, put much of their property into objects of permanent value. The working classes had no such skill, or foresight, or means. On them came, finally, the great crushing weight of loss."

Save war, there is nothing more devastating than inflation when it gets beyond control. Are we to permit it to get beyond control? If not, then the people must awake to the danger. For only through an aroused public opinion is there any hope of arresting the forces that, with all safety barriers down, will sooner or later gain irresistible momentum.

It is perhaps too much to hope for, but no effort should be spared to persuade the Administration and the Congress to adopt a fiscal and monetary program that will restore some of the checks which experience and prudence call for, and will furnish a mighty impetus to recovery by removing the fear and uncertainty that now paralyze business and enterprise. To that end we should urge:

(1) The repeal of the Thomas Amendment, which authorizes the President to issue greenbacks and to adopt bimetallism.
(2) Abandonment of the silver purchase program.

(3) A prompt return to an outright gold bullion standard, with a unit of weight not less than the present standard dollar.

(4) Cooperation with other nations in the international stabilization of currencies.

(5) Freeing the Federal Reserve System from political domination, and a restoration of its original functions.

(6) Termination of the present orgy of uncontrolled spending and adoption of a program looking to a balanced budget in the fiscal year beginning July 1, 1936.

(7) The return to a government of laws as contrasted with one of Executive discretion.

It's not too late to put our financial house in order. But, make no mistake about it. It's getting late.

December, 1934.

CHAPTER V

RECOVERY OR BUST

SPEAKING at Topeka last January, I said that our economic problem resolves itself into a race between business recovery and the exhaustion of the national credit.

Everything that has happened since confirms that opinion. When the cornerstone of the Administration's recovery program is government spending, when every major policy creates a situation calling for more and more spending, we either attain recovery, or bust.

As I then pointed out: "It follows that all unnecessary drains on the Federal Treasury should be avoided, and all avoidable obstacles to recovery should be eliminated." This has not been and is not being done. Quite the contrary.

MORE SPENDING—LESS BUSINESS

Today we are losing this recovery race. Government expenditures, already enormous, are rising day by day, with no corresponding increase in revenue. Expenditures the first quarter of this fiscal year were $1,517,-000,000, as compared with $923,000,000 a year ago. The *New York Times,* an independent paper friendly to the Administration, suggests that were economy the watchword, the expenditures for the last quarter might have been a half billion less.

By January, it is officially estimated that 20,000,000 people will be the recipients of relief—a new peak in the annals of destitution. Industrial production is much lower than a year ago and not much above the 1932 volume. Wages are higher, but real earnings have declined as a result of increased cost of living. Output per worker and per man-hour has greatly declined, and labor costs per man-hour, per unit of product, and in relation to gross income have sharply increased. The capital market is dead. The flow of credit has almost completely dried out. Construction and the durable goods industries are stagnant. The farmer grows more and more dependent on his government subsidy. The purchasing power of farm commodities in terms of goods bought by farmers is approximately the same as a year ago. Without the drought it would have been lower than a year ago.

In spite of infinitely greater resources, superiority in industrial equipment and efficiency of labor, we are being outdistanced by practically every other major country. In terms of the 1928 volume of production, industrial production in Denmark was 124 in August of this year; in Great Britain, 105; in Sweden, 103; in Norway, 102; in Italy, 91; in Germany 90; in Canada, 81; in France, 76; and in the United States only 69.

There's something wrong—very definitely wrong. While Washington won't admit it, thoughtful men and women everywhere are becoming increasingly anxious.

When all that makes life worth-while for every

member of this generation and the whole future of our nation are directly dependent on governmental policies, we would be guilty of unpardonable folly did we not make it our business to test the soundness of these policies in the hard, clear light of experience and of practical results.

It is in this objective spirit that I want to discuss our problems.

OUR AMERICAN ECONOMIC SYSTEM

The purpose of any economic system is to foster and maintain the prosperity of the nation and the well-being of the individual citizen. Generally speaking they depend upon the abundance of goods produced, their production at a cost that brings them within reach of the mass of the people, and their sale at such relative prices as will permit the constant flow of goods in exchange for other goods. Abundance of goods depends on the natural resources of the country, the industry of the people, the intelligence with which they work, and, above all, on the plants, tools and equipment with which they supply themselves. These, in turn, are the fruits of their creative genius and of their ability to accumulate savings.

Our American economic system has been remarkably successful in providing all of these essentials. It is a system of economic liberalism, of which freedom is the predominating quality—the freedom of individuals to follow any line of endeavor their tastes, capacity, energy and ambition may lead them to adopt; the freedom to save and to make such use of their savings as they see fit. A system under which the highest premium is placed on individual initiative, effort and creative enterprise. A system under which individual saving is steadfastly encouraged as the best means of assuring the productive capital essential to constant growth and progress. A system of automatic checks and balances, with the price mechanism as the principal governor. A system which lays great stress on the competitive process through which the economic organism cleases itself and achieves constant progress. A system under which, on the one hand, capital is constantly being accumulated and invested in creative enterprise; on the other, under the pressure of competition, new inventions and methods, obsolescence of plant, and changing conditions, other capital is being just as constantly dissipated. Though temporarily, individuals with accumulated savings actively employed enjoy great rewards, since all capital is inevitably consumed, in the long run the community is the sole beneficiary. The process of accumulation and dissipation is a continuous one. From it comes progress. Arrest it, in an endeavor to provide security for capital, and progress disappears.

GOVERNMENT REGULATION

Although this system lays great emphasis on economic freedom, as it grew in complexity greater intervention by the State was called for to prevent abuses by powerful combinations of interests attempting to exploit the public, and to maintain equality of opportunity. But, up to the present time at least, intervention and regulation by government have never proceeded to the point where they impair the motivating impulses, and violate the principles from which the system derives its strength.

GOVERNMENT MANAGEMENT

Substitute government compulsion for individual initiative and creative enterprise; discourage private saving; dam up the flow of capital; destroy the competitive processes; fix prices artificially; and, though you leave the ownership of private property undisturbed, and even attempt to assure profits, you will have hamstrung the American economic system.

Isn't that what's happened?

SUCCESS OF OUR SYSTEM

Now, whatever may be thought of some of these new collectivist systems, such as fascism, they have yet to prove their capacity to promote the welfare of mankind. Under economic liberalism in 150 years the world progressed further in terms of the well-being of average men and women than in all the previous centuries. Of all the nations, ours has moved forward fastest. We have enjoyed the highest standard of living and the greatest and widest diffusion of prosperity ever known in history. Generation after generation our national income has increased and the share of labor and salaried groups has grown greater. Generation after generation the standard of living has risen. Year after year the luxuries of today have become the necessities of tomorrow. One automobile for every five persons is an extraordinarily significant figure. We have been steadily moving forward to that ideal goal where the abolishment of poverty will finally be attained. Our march forward has several times been temporarily arrested. It always has been resumed, and carried to still higher levels.

WHAT CAUSED THE CRASH

But I can already hear someone say: "How about the crash that brought on this misery? Surely any system under which this is possible is defective." No man-made system is perfect. No man-made system is immune from the follies of man. In this particular instance the world-wide cataclysm of war distorted all economic relations, production prices, wages and channels of trade. It was followed by a reconstruction period during which all major countries committed errors of the first magnitude. Who was sufficiently wise to foresee the crash and to take measures to prevent it? When it came, the blow fell not on a firm structure, but on one hastily reconstructed, many parts of which were ill-adjusted and out of plumb.

The one demonstrable fact is not the failure of our economic system, but that the modern world cannot stand the shock of such a war.

In a healthy economic organism, the course of one of these depressions inevitably sets up counter forces that iron out the original causes of the depression and the ensuing maladjustments. In fact, if left to itself, in time the economic system would automatically effect its own cure. But under modern complex conditions, the social cost in individual human suffering would be intolerable. Therefore, government is compelled to intervene to cushion the fall, in the first instance, and to expedite recovery, in the second.

It fell to the lot of the last Republican Administration to perform the first function.

LIQUIDATION—THE FIRST PHASE

Political propaganda has painted the picture of an inert and inactive government. Nothing could be further from the truth. Immense efforts were put forth, immense sums expended to cushion the effects of the deflationary influences.

They included the expenditure of about two and a half billion dollars of public funds on construction work and the stimulation of the expenditure of hundreds of millions of private funds, the payment of nearly a billion dollars to veterans, the expenditure of nearly half a billion to support agricultural prices, the first great redundant credit campaign of the Federal Reserve System, the German Moratorium, the creation of the National Credit Corporation and later the Reconstruction Finance Corporation, the mobilization of private, municipal and Federal resources for relief purposes, and other measures too numerous to mention.

Mistakes were made. Some things were done which should not have been done. Others, desirable in themselves, the times did not permit. Still others, obviously necessary, were blocked by a partisan Congress intent on putting the Administration in a hole prior to election.

THE DEPRESSION HITS BOTTOM

In spite of this, the measures undertaken by the government and the natural forces of adjustment and recovery arrested the downward movement of business in the summer of 1932.

During that summer the bottom of the world business depression was reached. Industrial production turned upward, price deflation and credit contraction were arrested, unemployment ceased to increase, and world trade showed signs of recovery in all important countries.

True, we still had to weather the banking crisis of 1933. This, however, was but a comparatively short phase, albeit a wholly unnecessary one. I am not criticizing any man or group of men. But this I know to be true. If the Republican Party had been successful at the polls, or if Mr. Roosevelt had taken office in January, there would have been no banking collapse—though eventually the banking system would have had to be reorganized. For practical purposes, the Republican Administration terminated on Election Day, 1932. From that time, deprived of popular support, thwarted by a hostile and inflexible Congress, denied the cooperation of the incoming Administration, it was powerless to influence the course of events.

We had suffered terribly, but our social structure had withstood the strain. Tragedy had stalked through the land, but those in need had been cared for. We had suffered the full impact of a world-wide depression, but our constitutional form of government had been maintained faithfully; our dollar was still the soundest currency in the world; our industrial and economic systems, though weakened and still in need of treatment, were organically unimpaired. Though weak spots remained, immeasurably more had been eliminated. From now on, basic forces the world over would be pressing upward, not downward. The whole character of the problem had changed.

RECOVERY—THE SECOND PHASE

The first phase was over. The second, or recovery phase, was at hand.

The Roosevelt Administration took office under conditions which ambitious men, eager to make a record, would consider ideal. The bottom of the depression already had been passed. Circumstances lent themselves to a series of dramatic acts. The people had given an overwhelming vote of confidence. A Congress of the same political faith stood ready blindly to follow Executive leadership. The mere change in administration furnished a psychological factor of incalculable benefit. All that was needed to make success complete was a Recovery Program soundly conceived and fearlessly carried out.

While concededly there were long-time problems of immense complexity, most of these were not immediate, and could be postponed to smoother times.

A SOUND RECOVERY PROGRAM

The main elements of a strictly Recovery Program were fairly clear, provided we meant to work within the framework of our existing system.

The first job to be attended to was the clearing up

of the banking crisis and the restoration of our credit mechanism. No criticism can be made of the plan adopted as far as it went, though its execution left much to be desired.

Second. The placing of the credit of the government on an unassailable basis by bringing expenditures under control and working toward a balanced budget.

Third. A continuation of the Federal Reserve System's policy of extremely easy money.

Fourth. A solution of the immediate agricultural problem. Prior to and throughout the depression, prices of agricultural products were much below the general price level. They constituted one of the chief maladjustments in the general price structure. The causes were: excessive crops of certain staple products, lost foreign markets and diminished domestic demand. The ultimate solution is a long-time one. But temporarily relief could be afforded through the retirement of marginal or high-cost lands by a system of renting. Instead, the Administration elected to keep potential production alive by inducing, and later compelling, farmers to withdraw from cultivation good and bad land alike.

Fifth. A systematic thought-through program of unemployment relief, and creation of work, free from waste, graft and politics.

Sixth. A sound monetary policy, accompanied by an honest effort to establish world monetary stability through cooperation with other nations at a time when we still held some trump cards, and before repudiation had become both general and fashionable.

Seventh. An equally sincere effort to free the world

from those artificial creations that stifle world trade, and so regain lost markets. The chief obstacle to world trade has not been tariffs, but rather special import quotas, depreciated currencies, foreign exchange control, clearing agreements and the general tendency toward barter and mediæval mercantilism.

Eighth. Assistance to special classes of debtors such as home owners and farmers temporarily incapable of meeting obligations because of extraordinary conditions.

Ninth. Restoration of confidence on the part of investors by the adoption of a Securities Act based on the British model.

It is interesting to note that at one time or another nearly all of these measures were either considered by the Administration or actually undertaken, only to be distorted, abandoned or supplanted by the present ill-conceived program.

It should be further noted that, while many involved new interventions and departures, none did violence to the fundamentals upon which the American economic system is based, or to the motivating impulses from which it draws its energies.

WHY WAS THE SOUND PROGRAM REJECTED

An outsider can only speculate about the reasons which led to the change, but the following conclusions are not unreasonable:

REFORM VS. RECOVERY

In the first place, the Administration did not directly and vigorously address itself to the task of recovery, but emphasized what are known as the reform features of the New Deal.

It is just as if a doctor, called in to treat a patient, who had just overcome the crisis of pneumonia but was still sick, should begin by inoculating him against cold through the use of serums that further upset him.

FALLACIES

In the second place, there is abundant reason to believe that the diagnosis of some of the causes of the disease was far from accurate and that certain current fallacies were accepted at their face value. There is the fallacy of general overproduction and of attempting to cure want in the midst of plenty by doing away with the plenty. There is the fallacy that the increased purchase of goods for current consumption is of itself a powerful enough impulse to bring recovery, ignoring the fact that building and construction of all kinds, and the so-called heavy industries, which furnish the bulk of the unemployment, are the real key to recovery and that what they need is a capital market. There are the twin fallacies of the value of an artificial price rise, induced by monetary manipulation, and of the value of government spending for the sake of spending.

IGNORING FUNDAMENTALS

In the third place, I think the Administration either underestimated the importance of certain fundamental factors in our economic system, or determined to ignore them in an attempt to supplant our existing system with one of a different character.

How otherwise can we account for the suppression of individual initiative and enterprise by continued uncertainty; the limitation of production; the elimination of competition; the discouragement of saving by the threat to security of value and limitation of use; the restrictions on the flow of capital; the hamstringing of the price mechanism by the threat of inflation and by the arbitrary fixing of prices; and the wholesale regulation by government of all business, large and small?

Given these inhibitions, limitations and restrictions, our economic system cannot function. Though the patient may be kept alive by the constant use of stimulants in the form of government spending, this is not the road to health.

And should the medicine give out, then what?

We have seen what the program might have been. We have seen why it wasn't. Let us now take a look at what it is.

THE ADMINISTRATION PROGRAM

In broad outline, the recovery effort consists of four major policies: monetary manipulation, government spending, the N. R. A., and the A. A. A.

ARTIFICIAL PRICE RAISING

Monetary manipulation was undertaken on the false assumption that an artificial rise in prices would in and of itself do good. It does nothing of the kind. What is vitally important is not a particular price level, but such relationships between prices within the price structure as will permit goods to move freely from producer to consumer, always remembering that all producers are consumers, and all consumers producers. For instance, the fact that agricultural prices are low is nothing like so important as the fact that they are relatively much lower than the prices of manufactured goods. Some speculators may gain from inflation. Here and there some temporary advantage may accrue to producers and to a limited number of debtors. But the great mass of the people can only lose. The cost of living outdistances wages, thus reducing purchasing power. The value of savings is diminished. Uncertainty stifles enterprise. Capital grows timid. Business marks time. Employment decreases.

GOVERNMENT SPENDING

Government spending, provided the money does not come from taxes or from the transfer of savings to the government in the form of loans, but is new money manufactured by the government through the medium of bank credit, does create purchasing power and artificial business activity. But the purchasing power and the activity can continue only as long as the government continues to spend. The engine runs only as long as we feed it fuel. It's not enough just to start it. There is no such thing as perpetual motion. And even the artificial activity does not compensate for the normal activity and employment that would take place were it not for the disturbance and uncertainty created by huge deficits and constant borrowing by government. This gets us nowhere.

THE N. R. A.

The N. R. A., on a limited basis and with patience, might have done much good in the protection of labor and the gradual reorganization of our industrial machine. But the plan as actually conceived and managed has a heavy debit balance against it. Briefly stated, the theory was that if all business would undertake to shorten hours, increase wages and take on new men, the new purchasing power thus created would support an increased volume of business. It was putting the cart before the horse, but that was nothing in this "Alice in Wonderland" world of ours. It might work if costs and prices did not rise faster than purchasing power. It turned out to be a pretty big "if." They did.

Moreover, since all businesses, good and bad, inefficient and efficient, solvent and insolvent, were included, the weak brothers had to be helped if they were to join the party. So competition was suspended. The government encouraged price fixing. Costs and prices rose faster than purchasing power. Volume failed to materialize. The N. R. A. instead of promoting recovery, has retarded it.

THE A. A. A.

In view of the drought, the results of the agricultural program are hard to appraise. On the whole, the farmers must have benefited from the government payments. But even this benefit is temporary. It continues only as long as the payments continue.

What the government has done is to pay the farmer to keep out of production good and bad lands alike. The potential overproduction remains. This is a stop-gap. It's no solution, and there's no evidence of a long-time program.

ALL ROADS LEAD TO THE TREASURY

As I said at the outset, the heart of the entire situation is government spending. Deliberately or unconsciously, an artificial structure has been created which is wholly dependent on government credit.

When monetary manipulation or the N. R. A. forces prices up faster than the increase in current purchasing power, the Federal Treasury must close the gap; when the farmer curtails production, his income must be supplemented by a government subsidy; when business, deprived of its normal energies, shows signs of slowing down, it must be galvanized into artificial activity by a fresh outpouring of funds.

There are only three possible outcomes. We can continue as we are going, on the chance that the latent strength in our economic system, and world-wide upward forces, will pull us through in spite of it all. We can continue to the end of the road where the disaster of outright inflation awaits us. Or we can modify the program along the sound lines which I have outlined and which the Administration almost certainly once considered.

WHAT CAN WE DO?

What can you and I do? We can begin to do some clear thinking. Granted that no one ever shot Santa

Claus, is there any reason why the entire adult population should take to believing in him? Isn't it about time to realize that reindeer are not bringing these billions from the clouds, but that they'll be paid for either in taxes that will reduce the standard of living of all for a generation, or through an inflation that may ruin us as completely as it did Germany? Against all the teachings of experience, must we with blind faith continue to look to the government as our sole means of salvation?

This country of ours was not made by rulers or governments, but by a self-reliant people. The history of the United States is not the story of the accomplishments of government. It's the tale of the creative genius of a nation. This looking to government for salvation is a new-fangled doctrine for Americans.

The strength of this Republic lies not so much in the virtue of its rulers as in the common sense of its people. The time has come to apply some of that common sense.

We must make it our business to understand the situation and the nature of the problem. We must see to it that our neighbors do. When enough people do, Washington will begin to. We must think unselfishly, in terms of the common good, weighing each measure by that standard alone. It's not a question of what's good or bad for you and me, or for this group or that group, but what's for the good of all. Let's think for the common good, plan for the common good, organize for the common good. There is a way out. If the government cannot find it, let the people lead the way.

October, 1934.

CHAPTER VI

FINANCIAL POLICIES FOR RECOVERY

FINANCIAL Policies for Recovery, is so broad and comprehensive a subject that all one can hope to do is to sketch certain ultimate objectives which will in the main determine the broad lines of policy to be followed, rather than to attempt an analysis of the immediate steps to be taken.

Though unwise financial policies can retard its attainment, wise financial policies cannot of themselves bring about recovery. And they themselves must in large measure be determined by our fundamental attitude toward the main problem. In this, as in all major depressions, many intelligent observers, viewing the vast volume of raw materials and manufactured goods not moving into consumption, and the many idle plants, are so impressed by apparent overproduction and excessive plant capacity that they see in them the causes rather than the symptoms of the depression. From which they conclude that the true remedy is to be found in a limited and controlled production. Many instances of such views held in the past could be cited. One illustration will, however, suffice. In a notable report written in 1886, the then Commissioner of Labor, Carroll Wright, stated in part as follows:

"Industry has been enormously developed, cities have been transformed, distances covered, and a new set of economic tools has been given in profusion to rich countries, and in a more reasonable amount to poorer ones. What is strictly necessary has been done oftentimes to superfluity. This full supply of economic tools to meet the wants of nearly all branches of commerce and industry is the most important factor in the present industrial depression. It is true that the discovery of new processes of manufacture will undoubtedly continue, and this will act as an ameliorating influence, but it will not leave room for a marked extension, such as has been witnessed during the last fifty years or afford a remunerative employment of the vast amount of capital which has been created during that period. * * * The day of large profits is probably past. There may be room for further intensive, but not extensive, development of industry in the present area of civilization. * * * Supplying themselves with full facilities for industry and commerce will give to each of the great nations of Europe and America something to do, but the part of each in this work will be small and far from enough to insure more than temporary activity."

His estimate of the situation as it then existed coincides almost exactly with numerous appraisals of the problem which confronts us today. In my judgment, these present-day conclusions are likely to prove as erroneous as the earlier one.

In the meanwhile, this broad assumption that overproduction and excessive plant capacity are at the bottom of our troubles, is in the main responsible for two definite policies that are being vigorously pursued the world over. The first aims through a variety of devices to restrict the home market of each country to the products of domestic industries, a policy that receives further support from an intense nationalism, which aspires to complete national self-sufficiency. The second policy almost inevitably follows. The conception of a complete readjustment and reorientation of national economies calls for a degree of economic planning and control that can be exercised only by government, so that everywhere we are witnessing greater and greater bureaucratic interference and regimentation.

International commerce is being stifled. Production is reduced and rationed, and the standards of living are becoming consistently lower.

It is quite true that in any given industry, limitation of production, its allocation among the different units, and the maintenance of prices, irrespective of a lower cost of production by the more efficient units, may for the time being produce an appearance of prosperity in that particular industry. But, applied to all of the industries of a nation, such a process must end in national impoverishment, and, universally applied, must have a similar result on a world-wide scale.

On the other hand, if we study the history of the three-quarters of a century that preceded the World War, and consider the extraordinary and consistent growth in production, the steadily rising standard of living and a world trade that doubled every thirty years, it is difficult to be satisfied with a conception which accepts stabilization as a guiding principle, and in the face of well-nigh unlimited human wants for all manner of commodities sees even a temporary solution in their denial rather than in their satisfaction. We shall never solve the paradox of want in the midst of plenty simply by doing away with the plenty. Rather, should we devote all of our energies to the removal of those obstacles and maladjustments which present serious impediments to the exchange of raw materials and of finished products, both at home and abroad, and thus inhibit increased production, increased employment and a rising standard of living.

This means that in the world field, extreme nationalism, aiming at complete local self-sufficiency, should be curbed, and that those policies that are at present stifling international trade, such as excessive tariffs, quotas, exchange restrictions, etc., must be gradually relaxed. In the domestic field, we must insist on the restoration and maintenance of flexibility in our economic life.

I recognize that, in dealing as briefly as this with so large a subject, I run a serious risk of being misunderstood. But, even so, reference is necessary, for our decision as to which of the two courses we are to follow must have a profound influence on our financial policies.

For my part, I am prepared to cast my lot with the policy of what, for want of a better term, I may call economic liberalism, as contrasted with the rigidity of a controlled and regimented economy. If it be urged that this means a return to a system that has been tried and found wanting, my answer is twofold: First, the alternative proposed is a return to an even older system, a system that prevailed almost everywhere prior to the nineteenth century, and under which economic progress was measured in terms of centuries rather than decades. And, secondly, that the economic system under which the world made greater progress in seventy-five years than in all of the twenty-four centuries that preceded them, and which existed in its prime prior to the Great War, did not break down or fail us. The War tore it apart,—just as that same war destroyed empires, nations and institutions and well-nigh destroyed civilization itself.

It is true that the world post-war effort to rebuild that system fell short of success, but the foundations upon which we sought to reconstruct it were insecure, and our human architects proved fallible.

If, then, men and nations are to exchange goods and to trade on a constantly increasing scale, one of the first requisites is a common medium of exchange. To-day the growth of international trade is seriously hampered by the lack of one. Widely conflicting exchange rates and the uncertain value of currencies enormously enhance the risks and difficulties of doing business abroad. A return, therefore, to an international gold standard appears to be highly desirable.

Why a gold standard? As far as I am concerned, first, because I know of no system likely to function better. Secondly, because it is difficult enough to reach an agreement among many nations, and agreement on something which we know from experience facilitates the task. And, third, since we understand the functioning of the gold standard, and recognize its weak points, we are in a position to so modify it as to guard against them.

Much that has to be done to permit its restoration lies outside the monetary field, but there are certain monetary conditions that should be complied with. The more highly developed economic countries will need in every case a metallic reserve adequate to support a proper price and credit structure; it is essential that the central banks should cooperate more closely in the future than in the past, and should consider methods of control over abnormal movements of short-time funds; suitable measures will have to be established to prevent hoarding, and, finally, the gold value of domestic currency must be fixed at such points as will permit the maintenance of international equilibrium.

Notwithstanding its virtues, the gold standard has defects and weaknesses. It doesn't function automatically. It calls for a degree of management, and is, therefore, susceptible to human error and mistakes of judgment. But when established on firm foundations, its functionings are to a great extent automatic, and the field in which judgment operates consequently limited. These considerations carry great weight with me, for the past record of management offers no such picture of striking success as to encourage one to increase its scope at the expense of the more automatic process.

But, whether there is a gold standard or not, the control of credit and monetary systems involves difficult questions of policy and administration. To whom are they to be entrusted?

The maintenance of a stable currency and the pursuance of a wise credit policy are so essential to a healthy national economic life that there is a strong argument in favor of centering this responsibility in the State itself. In fact, the underlying conception that the issuance of currency is solely a function of government and a sovereign right that should not be delegated, recurs again and again in the history of our country. Nevertheless, in this and in all other highly developed economic countries, it has been deemed wiser to delegate the authority to control credit and to create money in the form of notes to certain special types of banks known as central banks—in the United States, to the Federal Reserve Banks.

The reasons are simple and persuasive:

The rate of discount is one of the most powerful means of controlling the volume of credit, and the rate of discount is properly the instrument of a bank.

Experience has demonstrated that in periods of stress, governments yield too readily to the temptation of financing their own needs by note issues at a time when such a policy may well run counter to the more fundamental economic interests of the nation.

Monetary policies and political considerations do not by any means run hand in hand, and placing responsibility in the hands of central banks is a convenient means of divorcing them. Incidentally, we are thus more likely to secure continuity of policy and of experience. For governments necessarily come and go. Under wise and prudent management, banks of issue do go on.

Finally, the government, as the largest individual borrower and lender, has a direct interest in the money market, and if charged with the duty of its administration, will constantly find itself in an equivocal position, where its own interests may conflict with a wise credit policy from the standpoint of the country.

These are compelling reasons for entrusting primary responsibility for the management of money and credit to central banks of issue. Nevertheless, money and credit are so intimately tied up with the general welfare that government cannot delegate complete responsibility and direction. It must reserve to itself some measure of supervision and control, and even of ultimate decision. The forging of this all-important link presents a very difficult problem of administration. There are a great variety of plans. In some cases, as in France, the government appoints the governor of the central bank. In others, as in Australia, the directors of the bank are appointed by the government. In Poland, the final decision rests with the Secretary of the Treasury.

With us, the task of coordinating the actions of our twelve Federal Reserve Banks, and to a very great extent of controlling their policies, is vested in the Federal Reserve Board, the members of which are appointed by the President, and of which the Secretary of the Treasury is the Chairman, and the Comptroller of the Currency a member. Moreover, certain members of the Boards of Directors of the Banks and the Chairmen of these Boards are appointed by the Federal Reserve Board.

We have heard and hear much criticism of our Federal Reserve System. Forgetful of the conditions which brought it into being, of its immense services to the country during the War, of its successful administration during most of the post-war period of reconstruction, and of the great advance it represents over the banking system or systems which preceded it, stress is laid on the failure to avert the disaster of 1929.

To hold the Federal Reserve System completely blameless would not accord with the facts. The corrective action came too late. This failure was partly attributable to the human element, and partly to the cumbersome character of the system itself. With the first we are not concerned in this paper. The second, however, deserves our thoughtful consideration.

Based on close observation for a number of years, my conclusion is that the Federal Reserve Board as constituted is not the most effective instrument for discharging the functions entrusted to it. The Board is too large to act promptly and with decision. With so many members, duties are so distributed as not to be sufficiently onerous to appeal as a general rule to active men. Living as they do in Washington, the members, upon whom rests the duty of final decisions, are out of touch with the swiftly flowing stream of affairs. Moreover, any difference as to policy between the banks and the Board frequently results in a stalemate, which may continue for weeks and months. In fact, this situation arises when the Board is equally divided, and so incapable of making a decision, no matter how vigorously the banks may clamor for one.

A Board of not more than three members might well be considered. An alternative proposal that has much merit would be to have a Board of five, composed of two Governors of the Federal Reserve Banks, serving in rotation for a year, two other members appointed by the President for life, and the Secretary of the Treasury. Such a Board would obviously have a much closer contact with current conditions and practical problems.

Under the first system above outlined, the Secretary of the Treasury should be a member of the Board, as, in my judgment, it is essential that there should be a close contact between the Treasury and the Federal Reserve System, so that both may be currently informed as to their respective policies and plans. I would not, however, give him a vote. But, in order to avoid the condition of stalemate which I have referred to, in the event of a serious difference of opinion between the Board and the Banks, I would allow an appeal to the Secretary of the Treasury, whose decision would be final. In view of the high character of men that have held this office ever since the early days of the Republic, I think we need have no misgivings as to the use that would be made of this power of final decision.

Under the alternative plan, I would make the Secretary of the Treasury a member of the Board, and give him a vote.

We have learned through bitter experience that for a country highly developed economically, such as ours, which makes the fullest possible use of credit in the conduct of all of its manifold activities, an unsound commercial banking system constitutes a fatal weakness.

Events have painted the defects in our commercial

banking system with cruel precision. If ever we are to learn and profit from past mistakes, now is the time. In a report which I made to the Congress, I summarized basic weaknesses and defects in our banking system as follows:

"1. During the 20 years ended with 1920 there was an enormous increase in the number of banks. In 1900 there were about 14,000; in 1920, over 30,000. In 1900 there was one bank for every 5,500 of the inhabitants of the United States; in 1920, one for every 3,500.

"2. This excessive growth in the number of banks was due in part to our dual system of State and National banks, and to a laxity resulting from its competitive feature. There is no doubt that both State and National authorities have in the past granted bank charters too freely, a condition to which the Comptroller of the Currency directed attention as early as 1927.

"3. During all of this period unit banking received every encouragement, while branch banking was discouraged and for the most part prohibited.

"4. The banking system of the United States as thus developed did not successfully meet the test of adverse circumstances. In 12 years there have been over 10,000 bank failures, or over one failure for every three active banks in the country in 1920. These failures have involved deposits aggregating nearly $5,000,000,000. They have brought untold hardship to countless individuals, and have intensified the economic depression.

* * * * *

"Various studies that have been made point to unescapable conclusions. The mortality rate is much greater among small banks than among the banks with larger resources. The earnings of most of the smaller institutions over the period of the last few years have been entirely inadequate, making it impossible for them to build up reserves. The cost of operation, and consequently the cost to the community which it serves, bears a direct relationship to the size of the bank. This is particularly true of the great number of institutions with limited resources that were operating in 1920 at the time the number of banks reached the maximum. The losses sustained by the smaller institutions have been relatively greater; and it is unquestionably true that a great number of the small banks have been unable to secure proper management.

"This does not mean that mere size will of itself guarantee good banking or a sound banking structure. These facts, however, do indicate that the operation of a vast number of independent unit banks under such conditons that it is difficult for them either properly to diversify their assets, to make earnings, to procure competent management, or to command adequate resources, is a definite source of weakness in the American system of banking.

"Our dual system and the divided control which exists have tended to relaxation in banking law and regulations, and to the development of unsound practices in the management of the banks."

My conclusion is that there can be no fundamental cure for such conditions until we are willing to create a unified banking system and to permit branch banking not on a nation-wide scale but within limits based upon actual economic conditions and credit needs.

Finally, we come to the fiscal policy of the government itself. The cornerstone of any sound fiscal policy must be an unswerving determination to return as rapidly as possible to the condition where receipts and expenditures are in balance. The healing and helpful influences of a stable currency, wise monetary and credit policies, a sound commercial banking system, and all the business confidence which they engender, may to a large extent be offset if the credit of the government can be brought into question. And the credit of the government will be questioned, not necessarily because of large temporary deficits, but if once the opinion becomes prevalent that the government is unable or unwilling to bring expenditures under control.

Moreover, there can be no doubt that one of the most important elements in our progress toward recovery is a resumption of the flow of capital into all manner of permanent and semi-permanent improvements. A plentiful supply of capital, low long-time interest rates, and confidence in the stability of the monetary system, are prerequisites to any such movement. As long as the government preempts the capital market for the financing of its own expanding debt, and as long as the fear exists that this process may continue indefinitely, conditions will continue unfavorable to the making of those long-term commitments that are so essential in any recovery program.

Do not misunderstand me. The government at whatever cost must meet in full its duty toward those who are in need. But there are many who would go further and who believe that government spending in and of itself is a distinct contribution to recovery. The danger is that these expenditures may be so made as to be incompatible with the expansion of private business and employment. And there is a further reason that has been clearly pointed out by Professor Sprague:

"I do not doubt that an increase in consumer purchasing power however brought about, will increase the immediate demand for many kinds of consumer goods. I do insist, on the other hand, that an increase in consumer purchasing power that arises from an increase in governmental expenditure runs the risk of creating a situation in which either this expenditure must go on indefinitely or, when it ceases, involve the same problem of readjustment that presents itself when Government expenditure is reduced at the close of a war."

In conclusion, you will observe that I bring to you no panacea. I know of none. For magic does not exist in the realm of finance any more than it forms part of any of the other realities of life. I have talked in terms of ultimate objectives. But I have the feeling that these, as well as many other desirable goals, may not be so far distant as they now seem. The world over, basic forces are working toward recovery. With patience, with self-restraint, with justifiable faith in ourselves, in our own experience, traditions and institutions, and with just a little more human wisdom and spirit of cooperation on the part of mankind, this generation will yet wake to see the dawn of a new day.

March, 1934.

CHAPTER VII

SOME ASPECTS OF THE MONETARY PROBLEM

You have asked me to speak on some aspects of the monetary problem. The heart of this question as at present discussed is the possibility and desirability of raising the domestic price level through monetary means.

There is much confusion in the public mind. It is an extremely technical question, that does not lend itself to an emotional solution expressed in terms of a desired result, but must rather be approached in a dispassionate mood, and with a willingness to do some honest thinking.

But, though technical and intricate, it can be reduced to certain essential facts that, if understood, will at least permit us to grasp the nature of the problem. I want to begin by stating these fundamentals as I see them, and then proceed to such elaboration as time permits.

First. The dominating element in our monetary system is the credit created and afforded through and by our commercial banks. We are a check-using nation, and 90 per cent of our business transactions are paid for by check.

Second. This credit system is the monetary factor

that at any one time predominantly influences the price structure in so far as it is influenced by money.

Third. This bank credit and check money element is self-created from without, and comes into being in response to business, industrial and commercial demands.

Fourth. There are two other important major factors in the monetary field. B, the basic gold reserve, and C, the resources made available to commercial banks by the Federal Reserve Banks, and I include under C the elastic part of our currency system.

Fifth. These factors, important as they are, can influence the price structure only by acting through the commercial credit mechanism, and are essentially long-time factors.

Sixth. Any attempt to affect the price level through monetary action which creates distrust and uncertainty will be restricted and may be nullified by limiting the normal creation of commercial credit, the mainspring of which is confidence.

Seventh. Efforts to raise prices through monetary action to date have been directed with a view to working either through B, the gold reserve factor, or C, the Federal Reserve Banks; that is, to force the creation of new credit from within rather than to promote its normal expansion from without.

Eighth. The steps taken have aroused the fear that they might lead to uncontrolled inflation, since the implication is always present that when moderate measures fail, extreme ones may be attempted.

This probably sounds to you like Chinese. Let us try to translate it into English.

Already we have witnessed a departure from the gold standard; the passage of the so-called Thomas Bill, with all of its inflationary features; the promoted and steady depreciation of the dollar in terms of foreign exchange; an enormous and growing government deficit; an immense volume of securities purchased by the Federal Reserve Banks; $850,000,000 of excess reserves in our commercial banks, the largest amount in history; and, more recently, a further depreciation of the paper dollar in terms of gold, through the sale of dollars abroad, and the acquisition of foreign exchange used for the purchase of gold at a price above that in the world market. All of these immensely important steps and measures have been accomplished by the threat and fear of uncontrolled inflation. And yet it can fairly be said that the unequal rise in prices in the domestic market is no greater than would normally have been expected to accompany a gradual emergence from the extreme bottom of a major depression.

There are very definite reasons for this failure. They are not simple questions, though someone more skilled than I should be able to explain them in simple terms. In any event, let us try.

Let us begin with the comparatively simple question of "What is Money?" In days not far distant, and during a very long period of time, real money, or, if I may so call it, primary money, was the gold coin. It had obtained undisputed eminence through ages of experimentation, and through the accumulated knowledge of the centuries.

But gold, of course, was not the only money, though

in gold standard countries other forms of money derived their value from the fact that they were ultimately convertible into gold. In the United States, for instance, we are all familiar with the paper currency and with the silver and copper coins that serve our daily needs. They consist, in part, of currency issued directly by the Treasury, which the Treasury under the law was compelled to maintain at a parity with all other forms of currency; and partly of bank notes, issued by the twelve Federal Reserve Banks against collateral, which included not less than 40 per cent of gold. We had, then, under the old system a comparatively small circulation of gold coins and a variegated assortment of paper currency and subsidiary coins, all maintained at a common standard of value because all were ultimately redeemable in gold coin.

This currency and these coins represented what we ordinarily call money. But in the practical working of our financial and banking system, they were a relatively small part of the actual money in use. In the United States approximately 90 per cent of the volume of business transacted is covered by checks drawn on commercial banks. Bank credit or check money is the most important feature of our monetary system. This is a central and all-important fact.

Some of our inflationist friends who insist that what we need is more currency misunderstand the position of the commercial bank in our monetary system. They visualize it as an institution whose primary function is to receive currency deposits from some for safe-keeping purposes and to loan it to others for business

purposes. Of course, transactions of this character
represent some of the business of banks, but the great
bulk of our deposits is created by the borrowing by
business men from banks for the purpose of carrying
on current business or commercial transactions. If A,
who runs a department store, borrows $10,000 from a
bank to finance the goods on his shelves until they can
be sold, he creates a $10,000 deposit. When, through
his checking account, he withdraws that deposit, it
finds its way to other banks in the form of deposits.
So that the original deposit remains in existence until
this or some other bank debt of a similar character is
repaid, resulting in a reduction of deposits by this
amount. It is through the continued creation and circulation of this immense volume of deposit currency,
running into many billions, that the business of the
country is transacted.

In this connection, one other very important factor
is to be noted. Important as is the total volume of
deposits, what is even more important is the velocity
with which these deposits are turned over. Thus, a
deposit of $1,000 that turns over twice does the work
of a $2,000 deposit, just as the thousand dollar deposit
that is turned over three times does the work of a
$3,000 deposit.

I do not want to leave with you the impression that
these deposits are just created out of thin air; that
there is anything unreal about them. They come into
being in response to a legitimate need for financing
some business transaction, and if the loan be sound,
are liquidated when the transaction is completed.

Aside from the presumably self-liquidating collateral behind each loan, and the responsibility of the borrower, what gives security to these deposits? Generally speaking, our commercial banks are obligated to carry 10 per cent of their deposits with the Federal Reserve Banks, and the Federal Reserve Banks in turn carry a 35 per cent gold reserve against deposits in addition to the 40 per cent gold reserve against their notes.

Under this system a dollar in gold in a Federal Reserve Bank can become $28.50 when transformed into a deposit in a commercial bank. We have thus at all times an almost unlimited capacity for potential credit or monetary expansion.

There is always great danger of inaccuracy in an oversimplified statement, but, for the purpose of this discussion, there are three main factors which you may consider as forming the picture. There is, first, the ultimate reserve held in gold. This constitutes a minimum 40 per cent reserve against note issues by the Federal Reserve Banks and a 35 per cent reserve against deposits with Federal Reserve Banks. At the present time the total amount of gold in the country is $4,323,000,000, an amount far in excess of the amount needed to support a much-increased credit and price structure.

The second main fact that you want to keep in mind is that the reserves of the commercial banks are kept in the form of deposits with the Federal Reserve Banks, and that a $10.00 deposit with the central bank will cover a $100.00 deposit in the commercial bank. The commercial banks today have with the Federal

Reserve Banks $800,000,000 more than they actually need in the way of legal reserves, which means that, without using any of their other resources, they could expand credit tomorrow by over $8,000,000,000 if there were a demand for it.

And the third, and most important, factor of all is the vast volume of deposits in the commercial banks through which the business of the country is paid for. Today they aggregate no less than 28 billion, in addition to almost six billion of currency in circulation, an amount in excess of that outstanding in 1929.

In so far as the monetary factor enters into the price structure, or, to put it more simply, affects prices, at any one time, it is the third factor above enumerated that is the all-important one.

Over a long period of time, the size of the gold base has an undoubted effect. Over a somewhat less long period of time, the Federal Reserve resources available to member banks for reserve purposes have an effect.

But it is to the total volume of commercial bank credit and the velocity with which it turns over that we must look for any increase in prices at a comparatively early date. That is the first important point I want to make.

The second is that since, as we have already seen, this bank credit or check money comes into being only in response to the needs of business, trade and commerce, and moves at a velocity determined by those needs, it will not respond to pressure from within, but expands and accelerates its turnover only in response to stimulation from without.

What the Government has done is to apply its

efforts to the first two factors. These have, generally speaking, failed, since they are at best long-time factors, and in any event reflect their effect only through the third factor. But, worse than that, in the process there has been created so much uncertainty and lack of confidence that obstacles have appeared to the creation of the very credit which they hoped to bring into being.

Let me illustrate what I mean by referring to three provisions of the so-called Thomas Bill. That Bill bestowed upon the President power:

(1) To compel the Federal Reserve Banks to embark on an open market program of unprecedented magnitude;
(2) To issue $3,000,000,000 in greenbacks; and
(3) To reduce the gold content of the dollar by as much as 50 per cent.

The essential features of (1) and (2) are the same. When the Federal Reserve Banks buy Government securities in the open market, they pay for them through deposit credits to commercial banks. Deposits with the Federal Reserve Banks constitute reserves which we have already seen may, in the hands of commercial banks, result in a credit expansion of ten times the amount of the reserves so created. But the mere creation of this potential expansion does not bring it into being. The excess reserves are created. The potential credit expansion is there. But, since business working from the outside does not call it into use, nothing happens. Hence we see over $800,000,000 of idle excess reserves today.

If the Government used greenbacks to finance current expenditures or to retire maturing government securities, the $3,000,000,000 so expended would eventually find their way to the commercial banks in the form of deposits. They would be redeposited by the commercial banks with the Federal Reserve Banks. Again, we would have an immense potential increase in credit; but unless the demand were there, again nothing would happen.

In the meanwhile, something does happen. Monetary manipulation engenders a lack of confidence, and the very measures intended to promote a credit expansion and a rise in prices contain at the moment of birth the seeds of their destruction.

Let me not be misunderstood. Ultimately, when from some totally unrelated cause or causes, a business or commercial expansion does take place, at that time this artificially overloaded credit base may be the cause of infinite trouble in the way of speculative inflation.

So of the devaluation of the gold content of the dollar. We must recognize that our present dollar has been devalued in fact, if not in law, accompanied, of course, by the repudiation of the most solemn obligations of the government. But the effect on the domestic price level has been insignificant. If we eliminate the price results affecting imports, in so far as the domestic purchaser is concerned, and the price results on relatively few exports sold in world markets, the actual effect of the legal devaluation of the dollar would simply be to increase an already completely adequate gold reserve. But between that gold reserve and the actual price level is the immense volume of currency and bank credit, which is the only monetary factor directly, as we have seen, related to prices. This cushion is so large and so elastic that only over a long period of time can the effect of the increased gold reserves make themselves felt.

This brings me to the last major point which I desire to emphasize. Whatever ultimate effects the major monetary policies, either proposed or actually under way, may have on our domestic price structure, their immediate effect is strictly limited, and in all probability more than offset by the drag they impose upon the expansion of long and short-term credit, without which no general price increase, or, indeed, no recovery can come.

Furthermore, they contain two inherent and very great dangers. Looking to the more distant future, they create a situation which might again involve us in one of those speculative and inflationary movements which we have such cause to regret.

In the more immediate future, they involve the threat of uncontrolled inflation. It is the history of these movements that those who have happily anticipated early and striking benefits find themselves irresistibly driven forward from failure to failure until, torn from all moorings, they are engulfed. Upon the evils of uncontrolled inflation it is unnecessary to dwell. Suffice it to say that history teaches that for all classes of the population, save the speculator, inflation is as devastating as war.

At this point, you may fairly ask: "What, then, would you do?" I would at once put in motion an

orderly and carefully thought through program looking
to a return to the gold standard. Though time has not
permitted any reference to the international phases of
the problem, I would do so because the world needs a
common and stable medium of exchange, and I know
of no other. I would do so because I believe basic
forces are working toward recovery, and that they are
being held back by lack of confidence, and fear as to
the ultimate value of the dollar. I would remove that
fear by restoring the dollar to an unassailable position.
I would do so because I believe that, with restored confidence, and with a continuation of the Administration's policy to rehabilitate our banking system, those
all-important bank credits which I have so emphasized
would begin to expand, and the vast volume of credit
available would flow into active use. I would do so
because I am convinced we must look to a capital
market and our capital goods industries to break the
present jam, and I am confident that the upward impulse is there. And, finally, I would adopt this program because I know of no other way to remove with
finality the unquestioned threat of ultimate devastating and ruinous inflation which the present forces
carry.

December, 1933.

CHAPTER VIII

EVOLUTION WITH AN "R"

I AM glad to meet with you young Republicans. There never was a period in my lifetime when our party was more in need of the vigor, the idealism and the courage of youth. We look to you young men and women to furnish the leadership, the devotion and the fighting qualities in the great battle that is to be waged for the preservation of American institutions, and of the liberty of the individual from the tyranny of government.

The Republican Party was born to save the Union. It must now go forth to battle to save the principles upon which the Union was founded.

I believe that if the process now under way is permitted to continue unchallenged, American institutions and civilization are in greater danger than at any time since the founding of the Republic. I believe that unless the people rouse themselves to what is happening, they may find themselves in the grip of a system alien in character and totally inconsistent with American traditions. I believe that the time has come for all those who still cherish American ideals and principles to rally to their defense without consideration of expediency or self-interest. I believe that disguised in the New Deal are measures not intended primarily to be either recovery measures or of a temporary character, but constituting definite steps in a major program looking to the ultimate setting up of a system of economic planning by the Government on a nation-wide scale, accompanied by control of industry and the regimentation of the American people. A study of the writings and speeches of the most influential group in the Administration, together with the events that have taken place since the 4th of March, 1933, present an almost conclusive case.

The time has come to present the issue fairly and squarely to the American people, and to let them decide whether they desire to sanction a program which inevitably means revolutionary changes in our government, institutions and civilization. The people are entitled to have the issue sharply drawn. They are entitled to complete candor from both sides.

There must be no repetition of the 1932 campaign, when the Democratic Party made certain specific pledges, practically all of which have since been repudiated, while the true purposes of the present Administration were concealed in obscure and equivocal language.

The truth is that, involving as it does, government control of industry and of the economic life of the nation and the regimentation of its citizens, the New Deal conflicts with fundamental principles upon which our government is founded, and to the extent that its philosophy overrides or supplants them, the process is a revolutionary one. We are not gradually modifying what we have. We are turning to something totally different.

That's why the historian of the New Deal calls his book "The Roosevelt Revolution." That's why Mr. Donald Richberg proclaims: "The long-discussed revolution is actually under way in the United States. There is no need to prophesy. It is here. It is in process."

This is the truth. It is equally true that this revolutionary process must end in the destruction of individual liberty, for individual liberty cannot long survive the death of economic freedom.

It's not a question of *"laissez-faire."* Even Professor Tugwell admits this. We are pledged to maintain equality of opportunity for all. Individual freedom does not imply its use either at the expense of the rights of others or of the community. Our system of individual initiative and control is subject to regulation by government, as witness the Interstate Commerce Act, the Food and Drug Act, the Banking Laws, the Sherman and Clayton Acts, the existence of the Federal Trade Commission, innumerable State regulatory statutes and the recent decisions of the Supreme Court in the Minnesota mortgage case and the New York milk case.

Nor is there any difference in legitimate objectives, immediate and ultimate.

We are all prepared to support proper emergency measures calculated to promote recovery. We all recognize that our policies must be directed to bring greater security and a more widespread well-being among the

great mass of the American people and that high
standard of living which their resources, their industry
and their intelligence entitle them to. We all recognize the need of finding a permanent solution for our
two major problems: unemployment and agriculture.
We all recognize the necessity of eliminating the
abuses and weaknesses that have been disclosed. The
Republican Party, if it is to survive, must be prepared
to present a definite program to meet these issues. I
am confident that it can and will.

It's not a question of aims and ideals but of method
and of philosophy of government. There are those who
believe that democracy has outlived its usefulness, that
the complex conditions of the modern world demand
planning and control, and that these can be furnished
only by an all-powerful government.

This is the Fascist conception.

On the other hand, there are those who insist that
the individual must remain master of his destiny, for
from the individual spring those creative energies to
which mankind must look for progress. This is the soul
and spirit of American institutions. Our people have
ever held that liberty is essential both to individual
happiness and to social and economic development;
that no man can be happy unless he be given full
opportunity to develop his aptitudes and talents as he
deems best; and that no nation can achieve a full
measure of progress and prosperity save under a system which gives the greatest possible scope to individual initiative, effort and ambition. This is the
lesson of history. This is the American creed.

It's because everything in me, all that I know and feel, tell me that regimentation means retrogression, not progress, and the sacrifice of some of the most precious rights this country was founded to uphold and preserve that I am convinced that the present program must not be permitted to furnish the foundation of future American life.

In the language of Governor Smith, "Let's take a look at the record."

The surest way to understand the Government program and all its implications is to turn to the writing of the man who undoubtedly furnished its underlying philosophy—Professor Tugwell. In his book, "The Economic Discipline," after discussing our existing comparatively free, though regulated competitive system, as contrasted with govermental control of industry, he wholeheartedly advocates complete government control. He proposes "a survey of the nation's needs for goods and services of all kinds, and a study of our present arrangement for providing them. Such a study would be the basis for undertaking such a rearrangement of present industries or such a control over their actions as would meet the criteria of the plan."

Dr. Tugwell lays down certain requirements necessary to the achievement of complete governmental control over industry:

1. "The flow of new capital into different uses would need to be supervised. * * * If there were a system of planning, * * * which allocated to specific industries capital sufficient to produce an amount of goods which would be taken by consumers at the price possible

with capacity production, and no more, prices could
be lower than they are at present. The surplus investment capital could then be assigned to other industries."

2. "Prices would have to be controlled."

3. Industrial associations are to be set up which must
   receive certificates of convenience and necessity from
   the Government, with authority to fix conditions of
   competition, maximum prices and minimum wages,
   working under a control board that would determine
   policies affecting "production, prices, division of
   markets, working conditions and the like." On this
   Board representatives of the Government would sit.

I call your particular attention to the following sen-
tence: "Their duties would consist in the clear and
definite transmission to the Board of the general plans
for industry which are worked out *by the Government
itself. These would concern consumption, production,
the necessary allocation of capital, and prices.*"

In other words, the Federal Government is to control our entire economic life, to determine what we
may produce and at what price our products may be
sold, what we may consume and in what quantities,
what we may earn, and what hours we may work. The
United States is to be transformed into a sort of Spain
of the sixteenth century.

The Professor foresees that legal and administrative
difficulties are likely to prove embarrassing, but he is
equal to the task of overcoming these obstacles. We
must set up, therefore, he says, devices "of a sort to
which business men will at first voluntarily agree, and
which, at the same time, contain no threat to the pub-

lic." The amazing thing is that by setting up the bait of the temporary suspension of the Sherman Act, our business men fell for the code device just as he had foreseen. A resourceful man, Mr. Tugwell!

I know that all this sounds fantastic, and that it seems unbelievable that anything like this can happen in the United States. And yet—it's already happened.

While the American people, eager and hopeful to escape from depression miseries, were blindly accepting everything offered them, these particular theories of this particular Professor have actually been written onto the statute books of the United States. They are now the law of the land.

We have seen that Tugwell's basic prerequisites to a planned and controlled economy are control of prices, wages, production and the flow of capital. The N. R. A., the A. A. A., the Securities Act and the Stock Exchange Bill, taken together and supplemented by the Government's fiscal program, have already placed control in the hands of Government. The noose is over our head. Are we to permit it to be drawn?

Under the N. R. A., the Government in effect controls prices and wages, and indirectly production, since it can forbid the entry into a particular line of industry of a new competitor or the expansion of existing plants.

There can be no doubt that under cover of the codes, prices are being fixed in a number of industries, totally disregarding the fact that a system of price fixing in competitive industries starts a whole train of consequences that must end in destroying economic freedom and ultimately our form of government.

Under the Bankhead Law, it controls production directly, even to the extent of limiting what an individual farmer may produce on his own farm.

Under the Securities Act and the so-called Stock Exchange Act, which goes way beyond regulation of the Exchange, the flow of capital is brought under government control.

In spite of an immense volume of credit seeking use, the Securities Act has created such a condition that it has become necessary to turn to the Federal Reserve Banks for working capital for industry. The law as originally passed was so thoroughly bad that it had to be modified, but not for a minute is Professor Tugwell's conception of the control of the flow of capital by government relinquished. It takes a new form in the so-called "Stock Exchange Bill." In effect, the four hundred and eighty thousand corporations in the United States, and any new ones that might be created, cannot obtain capital through the sale of securities through brokers or dealers except under such rules and regulations as the Washington bureaucracy may set up. The issuing of securities means acquiring and making use of credit—and what Tugwell's philosophy contemplates is to put the control and allocation of credit into the hands of government. That's not the way this country was built up. We might never have had the automobile if, acting under the political pressure brought by carriage makers, some bureaucrat had forbidden the investment of the necessary capital for the development of now our greatest industry, or the radio, if in his lazy judgment its possibilities were too visionary. Who are the best judges of whether a new industry should be launched or an old one expanded? The men who are devoting their time, their energies and their savings to the development of industry, or some chair-warmer in Washington who has never had any contact with business of any kind, whether he be taken from the campus of a college or direct from the political clubhouse?

To me it is one of the most amazing events in all history. Without consideration, without debate, in precipitate haste, a great nation is abandoning a system under which, say what you will, and in spite of recurring depressions, it has enjoyed for one hundred and fifty years greater progress, greater and constantly increasing prosperity, greater happiness and greater freedom than any nation, any time, anywhere. And for what? For a system of centralized, rigid, bureaucratic control of all industry that has never worked anywhere and at any time, and even during its brief period of trial here is already exhibiting every evidence of failure.

I have read Mr. Tugwell's books. Nowhere do I find that he has seriously faced the impossible difficulties of a centralized and completely controlled national economy in a country such as ours, or frankly recognized that it is totally incompatible with democratic institutions.

The evidence supporting his conclusions is shockingly inadequate. Apparently to him the most conclusive argument is found in the following statement: "For many years the technical task of devising plans for regulating our complex economic interests was too difficult to attempt. But today we know that this is no longer true, for Russia has shown that planning is practicable." It's a pretty sweeping assumption that the Russian experiment is a success when the standard of living there is still about the lowest of any so-called civilized country on earth—that is, barely above the subsistence level. But let that pass. What to me is a monstrous thought is that anyone should suggest that the regimentation which has been applied to a nation, which never has and does not today enjoy the semblance of freedom, should or can be imposed on this the most liberty-loving, individualistic, enterprising and intelligent people in the world.

There are innumerable examples of government regimentation throughout history. Invariably it has repressed the creative instincts of mankind and throttled progress. It has never worked. It isn't working in the United States today.

The N. R. A. has practically annulled the Sherman Law. It has injured the small business man. It is daily placing an additional burden on the consumer. Except in a limited number of industries, it has failed to improve conditions. It has retarded rather than helped recovery by putting up costs and prices before the attainment of volume. It is breaking down administratively.

The A. A. A. is admittedly ineffective, since resort is had to compulsory crop reduction.

The Securities Act and the general uncertainty regarding monetary policies have dried up the capital market so that the heavy industries, the principal source of unemployment, continue to mark time.

We were promised that if these experiments did not prove successful, they would promptly be abandoned. Yet what is happening? The A. A. A., with its plan for voluntary cooperation, does not come up to expectations. Resort is had to compulsion. The N. R. A. is found in practice to be inapplicable to the purely local business concern; and its compulsory features almost impossible of administration. Does that lead to more moderation? Ask the tailor in Jersey City who went to jail for pressing a pair of pants for thirty-five cents when the august code demanded a nickel more. True, the weakness of the Securities Act is so apparent as to require amendment, but a new control over the flow of capital and industry is imposed under guise of regulating Stock Exchanges. We have in the last few days heard talk of soft-pedaling the N. R. A. It has not proceeded beyond the talk stage. But, simultaneously Secretary Wallace demands more dictatorial powers under the A. A. A.

The abrogation of the air mail contracts without hearing or evidence, the indefensible Mellon persecution, and the case of the Jersey City tailor should serve as warnings to all of what may be expected when government becomes a government of men rather than of laws.

The case of the Jersey tailor should be read by every man and woman in America. It exemplifies the tyranny necessarily implied in any program of regimentation. The American Revolutionary War was fought and the Constitution of the United States adopted to free the individual from the tyranny of government. Today, if such incidents continue to be tolerated, "individual liberty" will be but an empty phrase, without life or substance.

There was no statute of the United States fixing the price of pants pressing. How could there be? There was no such statute of the State of New Jersey. There was a so-called Code, adopted by certain individuals not elected by the people or holding public office, approved by the Chief Executive. The Chief Executive could on his own initiative have re-written the Code as presented by the Code Authority, and by Executive decree fixed the price at which pants could be pressed.

This man went to prison, not for violating a specific criminal statute, Federal or State, but for violating an Executive edict or decree. Shades of Patrick Henry and of Thomas Jefferson!

This isn't theory or argument, or deduction. It's stark reality. I'm not talking of what might happen. It's already happened. What does it mean? It means that you and I and the rest of our fellow countrymen, pursuing with the utmost good faith the common callings of mankind, be they on the farm, in the factory, or in the marts of trade, doing only what we and our fathers had been accustomed to do, acts commonly accepted by the general opinion of mankind as not only harmless but beneficial, protected by Constitutional guarantees which had existed unchallenged for wellnigh 150 years, can today be sent to jail for violating an edict of the President, issued in accordance with a new philosophy of government never authorized by the people.

That, my friends, is tyranny. That, if one hundred

and fifty years of American history mean anything, is an assumption of authority that is revolutionary. As William Allen White writes:

"Our nation was set up for no mere material end or aim. We were founded to 'secure the blessings of liberty to ourselves and our posterity', and any scheme whether squinting toward Communism or at Fascism which tries to chloroform us to accept material security as the price of our ancient liberties, sooner or later will awaken us to the stark realities of despotism and its inevitable injustice and misrule."

In the face of this threat, what is the duty of the Republican Party? First and foremost, to proclaim its unswerving loyalty to American principles and American institutions, to invite all men and women who believe in them to rally to their defense, "and to preach the pure and undefiled doctrine of liberty under democracy."

We must be careful to distinguish between basic principles and policies. The former cannot be compromised. The latter must be approached with an open mind. In the light of new conditions, traditional policies must be reconsidered. The world moves. Immense changes take place. As a living organism, our party cannot live in the past. It must faithfully interpret the aspirations of the people by looking forward, by honestly recognizing defects in the existing system, and with equal sincerity seeking their remedy, and by rededicating itself to the task, in so far as it lies in the power of government to do so, of bringing to the great mass of the American people a more secure, a fuller and a richer life.

We believe that the promise of American life can be

fulfilled within the framework of existing institutions, without the destruction of individual freedom, and in accordance with the spirit and purpose of the founders of the Republic.

This is the fundamental issue that confronts the American people.

It cannot be compromised. It must be fought to the bitter end. With reverence for the past and complete faith in the future, we dedicate ourselves unreservedly to this task. For, in the language of Daniel Webster:

"Other misfortune may be borne, or their effects overcome. If disastrous war should sweep our commerce from the ocean, another generation may renew it; if it exhaust our treasury, future industry may replenish it; if it desolate and lay waste our fields, still, under a new cultivation, they will grow green again and ripen to future harvests. It were but a trifle even if the walls of yonder Capitol were to crumble, if its lofty pillars should fall, and its gorgeous decorations be all covered by the dust of the valley. All these might be rebuilt. But who shall reconstruct the fabric of demolished government? Who shall rear again the well-proportioned columns of constitutional liberty? Who shall frame together the skilful architecture which unites national sovereignty with State rights, individual security and public prosperity? No, if these columns fall, they will be raised not again. Like the Coliseum and the Parthenon, they will be destined to a mournful, a melancholy immortality. Bitterer tears, however, will flow over them than were ever shed over the monuments of Roman or Grecian art; for they will be the remnants of a more glorious edifice than Greece or Rome ever saw, the edifice of constitutional American liberty."

May, 1934.

The public authority (1) settled the price of raw material and the mode of using it; (2) banned any obnoxious industrial methods; (3) allotted masters' profits and workers' wages; and (4) could impose forfeiture of the right to follow a trade."

In 1231 Frederick II promulgated his economic policy of extreme paternalism. Monopolies were reserved, agriculture and internal commerce were regulated, and even model farms were established. In spite of his kind and benevolent intentions, a frightful despotism resulted.

Referring to Diocletian's experiment, followed as it was by those of his successors, Doctor Tucker succinctly summarizes the consequences: "Thereupon," he says, "there ensued a business depression that lasted for twelve hundred years."

EARLY REGIMENTATION IN ENGLAND

In England, as early as 1272, and for centuries thereafter, attempts were made to fix wages by statute, and even in the eighteenth century there were remnants of these futile efforts still on the books. Likewise, attempts were made to regulate the profits of merchants and other dealers by fixing the price of provisions and other goods. In 1815 the price of bread was still regulated.

The ancient guilds or corporations, operating under a charter from the King, but controlled by the towns, have much in common with our code authorities. They attempted to control supply, to control workers, to control the market and, quite naturally, prices.

In view of the protests now coming from our agricultural sections against the rising prices occasioned by the N. R. A. activities, it is interesting to read what Adam Smith has to say as to the relationship between these town monopolies and the agricultural districts: "Whatever regulations, therefore, tend to increase those wages and profits beyond what they otherwise would be, tend to * * * give the traders and artificers in the town an advantage over the landlords, farmers and laborers in the country." * * * Not much new in the world, is there?

SPAIN GOES "HAYWIRE"

Spain offers us perhaps the best example of a country where general stagnation of economic activity was brought about as a result of government control of private business. At the time of Queen Isabella, 1474 to 1504, the State undertook to plan the economic life of the country. The State sought supremacy at sea by paying premiums for the building and operation of large vessels. It succeeded in ruining owners of small vessels and reducing Spain's fleet to a few costly galleons.

It undertook to build up the merino sheep industry by prohibiting farm enclosures. This prohibition ruined the small farmers and with them Spanish agriculture.

The State fixed the prices of all commodities. The weaver, the potter, the shoemaker and all other producers were given definite instructions how to do their work.

It took an army of government officials to do the

supervising—all underpaid, most of them eager for bribes.

When the regimenters got through, Spain was done for.

FRANCE TRIES IT

In France, in 1664, under Louis XIV, his Minister, Colbert, undertook to establish national control of industry and commerce. Rigid governmental restrictions were laid down, covering the use of raw materials, processes, production, use of machinery, prices and wages. Great stress was laid on enforced standardization, which is particularly interesting in view of present-day efforts along that line.

In one of his letters, Colbert says: "The only means of rendering our manufactories perfect and of establishing a good system in our commerce is to render them all uniform."

JUST ANOTHER "FLOP"

The policy was a complete failure. The Government learned that State control meant State guarantee. Both workers and manufacturers insisted that if Government fixed the kind and quality of goods to be produced, it must make good the losses when the goods didn't move. Monopolies and subsidies followed. But, even so, the honest manufacturer found he couldn't compete with the "chiselers," who gave the public the goods they wanted at cheaper prices.

Colbert was undoubtedly an able man with broad vision and a high purpose. His planned and controlled economy failed under much simpler economic conditions than exist today, because he could not sense the essential value of freedom and because he made the same fatal error that our "brain trusters" do, of considering industry stable and static and, therefore, susceptible to control, rather than dynamic and in constant process of evolution, readjustment and change.

WHAT REGIMENTATION DID TO EUROPE

If we consider the state of Europe in the second half of the eighteenth century, we find a population of about one hundred and seventy million, the overwhelming majority of which lived on a bare subsistence level.

In Germany in 1800 the life of the laborer was no better than that of a slave. The average income of a Prussian peasant is estimated at twenty dollars a year.

At the end of the seventeenth century one-half of the population of England had an average family income of fifteen pounds or less per year.

The following poem describes the life of an industrial worker about the middle of the eighteenth century:

> "As negroes in Virginia
> In Maryland or Guinea
> Like them I must continue
>   To be bought and sold.
> While negro ships are filling
> I ne'er can save one shilling,
> And must—which is more killing—
>   A pauper die when old."
>   *The File Hewer's Lamentation*,
>   by William Mather, living 1737 to 1804.

A NEW WORLD IS BORN

In 1910 we find about four hundred and fifty million people occupying the same territory and enjoying, outside of Russia, a relatively high standard of living —certainly one infinitely higher.

As Mr. Keynes says: "What an extraordinary episode in the economic progress of man that age was which came to an end in August, 1914! The greater part of the population it is true, worked hard and lived at a low standard of comfort, yet were, to all appearances, reasonably contented with this lot. But escape was possible, for any man of capacity or character exceeding the average, into the middle and upper classes, for whom life offered, at a low cost, and with the least trouble, conveniences, comforts, and amenities beyond the compass of the richest and most powerful monarch of other ages."

HOW COME?

What had happened during these hundred years to bring about this extraordinary progress, to enable the same territory to support almost three times as many people as before on the basis of an infinitely higher standard of living and to permit England, for instance, to increase its national income twelve fold?

The coming of the machine age and the astounding technological development, you will say. Are you quite sure we must not go deeper than that? Why, after some eighteen centuries of comparative inactivity, should man's creative and inventive genius suddenly come to life and with such vigor?

Remember that a Roman of the time of Augustus suddenly transported to the England of the eighteenth century would, except for gunpowder and printing, have found little to surprise him. He would have been familiar with the great buildings, the fine roads, the means of transportation by land and water, agricultural processes and the various handicrafts. The world had stood still for eighteen hundred years. A hundred years later he would have been stupefied.

What had happened? Man's mind and imagination had not improved, as witness the comparative state of the arts. His nature and character had not been transformed. What, then, all of a sudden had loosed his creative genius?

I can give the answer in one word—freedom—political and economic freedom.

EXIT PLANNERS—ENTER FREEDOM

In 1776, two events of transcendant importance occurred: the American Declaration of Independence and the publication of Adam Smith's "Wealth of Nations."

The American Revolution and the adoption of a Constitution which guaranteed the individual from the tyranny of government, had an immense effect. With the coming of the French Revolution and, paradoxical as it may be, the onsweep of the French National Armies, the spirit of liberty swept Europe. The old order was dead. The planned and controlled economies went to join that of Diocletian. The heavy hand of government gradually relaxed its hold upon the lives of men. Within three-quarters of a century political freedom had been won in most countries, and economic freedom everywhere save in such backward countries as Russia.

The world bounded forward, after eighteen centuries of stagnation. Mankind enjoyed greater general well-being than at any time in the history of the race.

That all progress is born of individual effort, and man's dynamic energy and creative genius flourish only in an atmosphere of freedom had been proved beyond doubt. How otherwise can you account for the fact that when technological improvement came with giant strides, it originated in those countries where the economic freedom of the individual was greatest—the United States, England, France and, later, Italy and Germany? From Russia and Spain, where the old order prevailed, came nothing.

In the face of this record, we are turning back—back to the Middle Ages and to economic despotism! What a monstrous perversion of the word "progress"!

u. s. a. 1801-1925

And now let us glance at the history of our own country under a system upon the ruins of which we are supposed to build a new and better world:

In 1801 the United States had five million three hundred thousand people. Their principal occupations were fishing and agriculture. They wore homespun clothes and their housing, implements and other equipment were of the simplest kind. The standard of living of the masses was low. Wage-earners worked from sunrise to sunset, and their daily wage was about forty cents.

The situation of the people one hundred and twenty-five years later had been transformed—so completely transformed that the change hardly lends itself to statistical measurement. The comforts and luxuries of a highly developed civilization had come within the reach of the moderately well to do, while better food, better housing, better clothing and a vast increase in comforts and conveniences had been made accessible even to the economically less fortunate groups.

The progress eludes statistics, but they may, nevertheless, illustrate some aspects of the progress made in a hundred years:

In 1820 wages paid to American workers were 28 per cent of the 1913 average. The cost of living, on the other hand, was 65 per cent of the 1913 average. During this period the population increased twenty times, wages almost quadrupled, but the cost of living increased only 50 per cent. Thus, real wages increased two and one-third times.

During the same period the hours of labor were shortened, educational opportunities were broadened, and comforts that were formerly thought of as unattainable luxuries came to be regarded as ordinary necessities of life.

From 1863 to 1913, production of all manner of goods increased eleven times, and per capita almost four fold. Their increasingly wide distribution among all classes of the population accounted for a standard of living rising constantly generation by generation.

National wealth increased from some seven billion in 1850 to one hundred and eighty-six billion in 1912, or six and one-half times the increase in population.

DISTRIBUTION OF NATIONAL INCOME

The people are told in sensational propaganda and in speeches of agitators that, while all this may be true, the wage earner gets an inadequate share of the national income, that his share is steadily decreasing, and that three or four per cent of the population enjoy seventy-five to ninety per cent of the national income.

Recent official publications have torpedoed these false claims.

LABOR'S SHARE

In 1850 salaries and wages took less than 36 per cent of our national income. In 1909 the share of labor was 50 per cent. In 1929 labor income, including salaries, compensation, pensions and the like accounted for 63.6 per cent of the national income. By 1932 it had increased to 80.1 per cent. But from 1929 to 1932, the aggregate of labor income declined 40.3 per cent. The balance of income produced went to proprietors of farms and other business enterprises, independent professional persons, recipients of interest, rents, royalties, and to stockholders. The aggregate of their income declined 74.1 per cent in this same period, from 1929 to 1932. Actual payments to these groups, furthermore, had to be made out of capital and surplus, that is, by drafts upon previously accumulated assets. In some industrial divisions the payments made to labor were greater than the income produced. This was true in 1932 of the manufacturing industries, the construction industry, the mining industry, and trade.

CAPITAL'S SHARE

On the other hand, the share of all capital of all corporations in the country has not exceeded five per cent of the total values produced by them in the fourteen-year period, 1919 through 1932. Of this a substantial amount was not distributed to stockholders but devoted to increased productive capacity.

I do not mean to imply that we should by any manner of means rest satisfied with what has been accomplished. There are plenty of weaknesses and abuses to be cured. We must, can and will do much better in the future in so far as the general well-being is concerned. In particular we must learn through greater knowledge, wisdom, foresight, better organization and self-control to avoid these terrible periods of retrogression.

But I do insist that, in the face of these colossal achievements, we would be a mad nation indeed were we to abandon the system that has brought us greater happiness, greater prosperity and greater progress than have ever been enjoyed by any nation in all history in favor of a system that has been repeatedly tried and ever found wanting.

NORMAL OR ARTIFICIAL RECOVERY?

Finally, let us consider in terms of the present depression whether recovery has come fastest in those countries which have relied on normal recuperative forces and tried and tested policies or in those where resort has been had to all manner of artificialities.

But, first, let me make one point entirely clear. It isn't a question of *"laissez-faire"* as opposed to government regulation. Everyone knows that *"laissez-faire"* hasn't existed in this country for years. A system of regulation has been developed, intended to give business liberty without license. The issue is rather whether we are to reorganize the business and industry of the country by substituting detailed bureaucratic control in the place of regulated individual control.

Nor is it a question of a "do-nothing" policy, as contrasted with affirmative efforts to promote recovery. All the propaganda to the contrary notwithstanding, in the first years of the depression, colossal efforts were made under the last Administration to arrest the downward sweep. Whatever they may have done to cushion the fall, they failed to arrest the overwhelming momentum of the downward forces. These forces, however, had definitely spent themselves by July, 1932.

THE DEPRESSION HITS BOTTOM—JULY, 1932

The low point of the world business depression was reached in the summer of 1932, when industrial production turned upward, price deflation and credit contraction were arrested, unemployment ceased to increase, and world trade showed signs of recovery in all important countries of the world. This upward movement continued in the rest of the world, while our Presidential election and the uncertainty concerning the monetary and other policies of the incoming Administration caused another decline in our business activity, led to a flight of capital from the country, hoarding of currency and gold, and a banking panic. From March to July, 1933, while the rest of the world was steadily recovering, we experienced an unprecedented and thoroughly unsound spurt in business activity, caused by wild speculation in the stock and commodity markets following the depreciation of the dollar and by the introduction of the N. R. A., with its threat of higher production costs.

PROGRESS EVERYWHERE

In July our index of industrial production, 1928 being equal to 100, stood at 90. Then the bubble burst. In November it was 65.8, as compared with 58.6 in November, 1932, and the low point of 52.3 in July, 1932. It is significant that in October, 1932, the index number of production was only five points lower than in November, 1933, one year after the election of the present Administration. While we were experiencing these ups and downs, business recovery in other countries continued at a steady pace. At the end of the year 1933, industrial production in Great Britain amounted to 99 per cent of the 1928 average; in Sweden, 97.1 per cent; in France, 83.5 per cent; in Germany, 74.5 per cent; in Canada, 72.2 per cent; and in the United States, 67.6 per cent. During the first quarter of this year our production turned upward again in line with the world-wide trend. In Great Britain the volume of production at the end of the first quarter of this year was highest since the post-war boom. The British budget shows a large surplus. British capital issues for domestic and international account are rising. The long-term rate of interest has been reduced to below the pre-war level. London is again supreme in international finance.

In Sweden the volume of production in the first quarter of 1934 was larger than the average in the good years 1925-29. In Germany and Canada there was a sharp upturn which brought industrial activity in March to the highest point since recovery began. Australia is staging a remarkable recovery, as indicated by foreign trade, employment, bank clearing and governmental financial figures. Expenditures and taxes are being reduced, and the capital market has revived.

The conclusion that can be drawn from this brief analysis is that the recovery has taken place in all countries regardless of the existing economic and political systems and regardless of any specific governmental policies.

The recovery has been best sustained in those countries where the principles of liberal capitalism have been violated the least.

SOME SUGGESTIONS FOR RECOVERY

Today it is clear, in the light of what is happening the world over, that reasonably prompt recovery is within our grasp if only we will follow a course dictated by common sense and experience:

(1) Abandon the effort to impose on the American people the alien system of a planned, controlled and regimented economy.

(2) Give the normal forces of recuperation a chance by doing away with the uncertainty occasioned by continuous experimentation.

(3) Provide for the unemployed through State and local organizations, supplemented by Federal funds while working out a sound and permanent system to mitigate in the future the hardships of unemployment.

(4) Bring relief to agriculture by promoting the reopening of lost markets, and cooperation with the rest of the world in stimulating world trade and a rising standard of living the world over.

(5) This in turn means modification of tariff policies, the doing away with quotas and exchange restrictions and the reestablishment of a common medium of exchange—that is, a modified gold standard.

(6) Stop monkeying with our currency system.

(7) Restore the capital market by modifying the Securities Act and the Stock Exchange Bill so as to limit the former to the reasonable protection of investors and the latter to the regulation of the speculative markets. Let private capital go to work that men may go to work.

(8) Strengthen our banking system by working steadfastly for unification.

(9) Stop trying to squander our way out of the depression. Cut expenditures and dismiss from the public payroll the horde of unnecessary employees, to the end that the budget may be balanced, taxes reduced, and the sinking fund made once more operative.

(10) Retain the good features of the N. R. A. by doing away with compulsion by restricting its operations to truly national enterprises, and, while maintaining the Sherman Law on the Statute Books, permitting business associations to adopt rules for their own guidance subject to regulation in accordance with law.

(11) Make our Government once more one of laws and not of men.

Above all, in the name of progress, let us not turn back to an age-old and discredited system—the very system against which our forefathers revolted when they brought into being a new nation and dedicated it to the cause of human freedom.

May, 1934.

CHAPTER X

UNEMPLOYMENT RESERVES AS A STEP TOWARD GREATER INDIVIDUAL SECURITY

THE last five years have been tragic ones for many million American families. They have been unable to secure employment. They have seen their savings melt away; and a future, they had thought secure, grow uncertain. They have begun to lose faith in themselves and in their institutions. Their doubts are not justified.

The foundations upon which this country has been built are sound. The fundamental principles which have ever guided our steps still hold good. We shall emerge from this depression, as we have emerged from depressions in the past, just as certainly as the sun will rise tomorrow. The march forward will be resumed, as it always has been. Even in these dark hours, the promise of American life still holds good.

But the insistent demand for greater individual economic security, which we hear on all sides, will persist and must be heeded. It is a just and legitimate aspiration.

There are fields in which accomplishments along this line are definitely within reach. And beyond them I can visualize ultimate possibilities which, with patience and foresight, are not unattainable.

With the latter we are not concerned just now. I propose to confine my suggestions to one of the fields in which a greater measure of security may unquestionably be had.

Some twenty years ago, as a Member of the State Senate, I introduced a bill providing for the investigation of so-called social insurance. The move was premature. Nothing came of it. It is too bad. Had we had the wisdom to initiate at that time, on however modest a scale, a system of unemployment reserves, we would have built up during fifteen years of prosperity reserves that would have helped materially during the initial stages of the depression, and, what is perhaps more important, we would now have at our disposal invaluable experience.

As it is, it is undeniable that circumstances are unfavorable at this time. They are unfavorable, since neither industry nor labor is so situated as to make the building up of unemployment reserves an easy task; industry, because profits are lacking; labor, because earnings are inadequate.

Moreover, conditions being what they are, the people, anxious for a more orderly method of meeting human needs, and looking for immediate results, will almost inevitably tend to confuse relief proper with any system of unemployment reserves, or insurance, that may be set up.

I cannot emphasize too strongly that the two problems must be dealt with separately. The British experience is conclusive on this point. No practical system of unemployment benefits—even if reserves had previously been built up—is adequate to cope with the general unemployment resulting from a major depression. The attempt, by the application of insurance principles, to cover all phases of unemployment, however widespread and protracted, is bound to result in failure.

Nothing could be more unfortunate, from the standpoint of the success of any system or systems of unemployment reserves, than their confusion in the public mind with our present relief problem.

The latter we must work out as best we can, and I may add in passing that, once waste, politics and the notion that government spending *per se* is a help to recovery, are eliminated, all those in need can be cared for without constituting too heavy a drain on our resources, or causing a budgetary crisis.

Looking to the future, I am hopeful that modern knowledge, skill, technique, our amazing amount of current information and our means of disseminating it widely and rapidly, if intelligently availed of through cooperative effort, may tend to minimize the momentum of these mass movements which produce alternately peaks of unhealthy expansion and the deep valleys of depression.

But until that day comes, I believe that, after our present tragic experience, the people will demand more adequate provision in advance for meeting those relief needs, which because of the magnitude of a business recession, exceed the ordinary resources of our private agencies, municipalities and States. I am here talking of relief proper.

In this connection, I suggest that as soon as recovery has advanced far enough to warrant it, our State Legislature and municipal authorities make continuing appropriations, that the proceeds be placed in a special fund or funds until the funds reach an adequate size; and that the funds be invested in the bonds of the State and municipalities respectively.

This would mean that public debt would be decreased during periods of plenty; the governments placed in possession of additional borrowing power for relief purposes in periods of scarcity, and the necessity of imposing new taxes, at a time when they are least bearable, avoided.

Reverting to the main subject, if then, an unemployment reserve system must be distinguished from the problem of relief, and if it cannot provide for all phases of unemployment, what definite benefits may be derived from the establishment of such a system or systems? I believe that unemployment reserves will furnish a first line of defense to the unemployed worker; will make provision for casual and intermittent unemployment; will stimulate constructive efforts to stabilize employment; and, while not supplying absolute security, will within limits give the worker greater security than he enjoys today, and satisfy, in part at least, a legitimate aspiration.

By providing unemployment income, for a stated period, to the worker as something he has earned by reason of his previous employment, unemployment benefits do much to give the worker a sense of security and to preserve his morale and self-respect. Instead of being compelled to apply for public help as a destitute person, the worker receives benefits as his right. They are an encouragement to thrift and steadiness, while relief is not. Relief frequently results in destroying self-respect in the individual. A system of unemployment reserves, on the other hand, built up and organized in advance, provides a planned and orderly method of assisting the worker, to which he may look forward with a feeling of assurance.

It is quite true that the setting up of reserves will reduce current purchasing power, and the bottom of a depression is, therefore, an inappropriate moment to launch the system, but the principle of creating reserves to give greater security to workers is in line with the sound policy followed by business of making provision out of current earnings for meeting future contingencies and for stabilizing the income of stockholders. Now, or at a comparatively early date, the establishment of such a system would not only be just, but wise.

The first question that arises is, whether an unemployment reserve system should more properly be set up by the Federal Government or by the States. I am convinced that the latter are the appropriate agency.

Looking at the matter from the standpoint of general public policy and fundamental principles of government, I am one of those who believe that the strength of our whole governmental structure depends upon the vigor and vitality of our State and local governments. This country of ours is too big, its interests too diversified, to be ruled from a single center. In a democracy, the closer the government to the people, the better the government. In spite of modern inventions that have done so much to reduce distance, Washington is still far off. Centralization, in my judgment, has already proceeded to the danger point. If we go much further, our State governments will become mere shadows, and the individual citizen will tend more and more, as, in fact, he is already doing, to look to Washington for the solution of all his problems.

The problem of setting up a system of unemployment reserves raises this fundamental issue in acute form. Here is a measure that will intimately affect the life of the individual and the interests of every individual industry. If it properly belongs within the jurisdiction of the Federal authority, then, as a practical matter, there can be no limit to that authority.

Conditions of employment, wages, standards and modes of living, differ widely in different sections of the United States. There is almost as wide a divergence in the character of the problems of the many diversified local industries that exist throughout the United States. The existence of our State governments is a recognition of these divergences and differences. Success is much more likely to be achieved by the recognition of conditions as they actually exist, and by permitting our States to solve this problem in accordance with the needs and wishes of their own people than by ignoring actual conditions and attempting the application of a single rigid and unified system.

The immense difficulties which the Federal Government has encountered in the handling of the relief problem is an example of the almost insuperable obstacles that would hamper successful administration if attempted from a single center.

There are two arguments that are advanced in favor of Federal action. The first is the time-worn argument employed by all zealous advocates of reform,—that action by the several States is altogether too slow and that the time element justifies the Federal short cut. I have never been impressed by the validity of this argument. When public opinion in this country has reached the conclusion that a particular measure of reform is desirable, action by the State governments follows with amazing rapidity, as witness the rapid spread of workmen's compensation legislation and, more recently, the speed with which the Federal Prohibition Amendment was disposed of.

Then, there is the argument that the States that are slow to act would gain a competitive advantage over their more advanced brethren. Whatever appeal this argument may have for people in other states, we in New York should know better. New York has led the country in social legislation, and yet has maintained and strengthened its industrial supremacy.

I think it is generally agreed among all those who favor the establishment of a system or systems of unemployment reserves that they should be compulsory in character. While voluntary action by a number of industrial establishments has yielded satisfactory results, progress along this line would of necessity be slow. If the principle is sound, then the application should be general, and the only way to make it general is to provide for it by law.

Coming, now, to a somewhat more detailed examination of the problem, we find that there is a fundamental issue upon which advocates of the various plans which have been suggested differ fundamentally.

There are those who support the European system, exemplified in this country by the Ohio Plan; and there are those who support the so-called American System, which has taken form in the Wisconsin Plan.

The Ohio Plan follows, in general, the unemployment insurance systems operating in most of the European countries. It is based on the assumption that unemployment is an insurable risk; that the risk should be spread among all those participating, by having contributions paid into, and benefits paid from, one central pooled fund; and that the primary value of a system of unemployment benefits is in the relief provided, rather than in the incentive to stabilize employment.

The chief feature of the so-called American Plan is that of separate unemployment reserves for each industrial establishment. Its advocates urge that it affords an important incentive to employers to stabilize employment; that it more fairly spreads the cost of unemployment benefits; and that it is more acceptable to the American industrialist.

The American Plan, as Professor Commons and others have developed it, has been endorsed by a majority of the State Investigating Commissions that have so far reported on unemployment insurance; and by the Interstate Commission, composed of the representatives of the Governors of New York, Massachusetts, New Jersey, Ohio, Pennsylvania and Connecticut, who met in 1932 at Governor Roosevelt's suggestion.

Based on such studies as I have made, though I am in no sense an expert, I am not convinced that actual experience justifies the assumption that unemployment among practically all classes of wage-earners is an insurable risk. If this be so, ought we to erect a system which will stand or fall according to the validity of this basic assumption? Isn't it much wiser to avoid the risk of failure by proceeding cautiously, by building step by step on a secure foundation, and by not attempting too much at the start in what to us is a wholly novel field?

Moreover, it is undeniable, because of the variation of risks between different industries, that a single pool with flat-rate contributions gives rise to all manner of inequalities. The British experience is fairly conclusive on this point. Sir William Beveridge, a noted British authority, referring to the distribution of contributions and benefits among thirty-three British industries, points out:

"Remarkable differences between the experiences of the different industries are at once apparent. Looking first at the figures for 1929, we see at the top of the table industries paying in three or four times as much as they draw out, and at the bottom of the table other industries drawing out three or four times as much as they pay in. The top eight industries with 1,305,000 workpeople draw out between them practically the same amount as 'dock, harbour, river and canal service' with 171,000 workpeople, while they pay in ten times as much; for every £11 paid in by the last industry towards the cost of its unemployment in 1929, £31 was found by other industries directly, to say nothing of £17 found by the taxpayer. Between the extremes is every possible gradation of experience."

It is quite true that attempts are made, as in the Ohio Plan, to iron out these inequalities by varying the premium rates levied on employers in accordance with variations in the unemployment index of their respective industries. But here, again, we are resorting to a complex element which involves a number of incalculable consequences, and which seems out of place in a system which, for some years at least, is bound to be experimental in character.

It is this same desire for simplicity that leads me to favor the suggestion made by the Connecticut Unemployment Commission in December, 1932. The Connecticut Commission suggests that every employer dropping a man for lack of work shall be obligated to pay him for a given period of time an unemployment wage. These payments would be similar to the benefits provided for under other systems. The fundamental difference is that they would be paid irrespective of whether the man found other work or not.

At first sight, the suggestion that a man should enjoy unemployment benefits at a time when he might have secured other employment is rather startling, and the possible duplication of payments appears costly. As to the element of cost, the Commission has this to say:

"Offhand, it would seem that the dismissal wage plan would be the more costly of the two. The Commission believes this would not prove to be the case. To the actual cost of unemployment benefits under the insurance plan, would have to be added additional costs, involving both the state and employing units. The state would have to maintain a complete system of employment offices accessible to every place of employment in the state; an elaborate system for registering all employees; and be prepared to act in a judicial capacity between employer and employee, handling countless claims with their consequent hearings. The employing units would have the cost of making investigations of rumors that a dismissed employee had obtained employment elsewhere, as well as the cost of attending hearings. The Commission is convinced that it would involve far less financial drain on both the state and employing units to pay straight dismissal wages, even realizing that in a certain proportion of the cases the wage earner would be drawing his dismissal wage and earnings on a subsequent job at the same time."

What appeals to me is the simplicity. Under the other plans, it is necessary to set up complicated machinery to check the ability of the unemployed worker to find other work, to determine whether the work is suitable, and to solve other similar problems arising in connection with the termination of benefits. Anyone who has studied the British system appreciates the complexities that necessarily arise. And with us there is always the danger that politics would creep into this complex administrative machinery, and that favoritism and pull would exercise the baneful influences with which we are only too familiar.

From the standpoint of the worker, I can see no objection to the plan. In so far as the employer is concerned, it would furnish a real incentive to stabilize employment, to spread work when production is being curtailed, and to re-employ his regular employees at the earliest possible opportunity.

Again, there is division of opinion as to whether both employers and employees should contribute to the fund. On the whole, it seems to me wiser that employees as well as employers should contribute. Employee contributions will permit larger benefits and a longer period of payment. They will give the workers a direct interest in conserving the fund and in keeping the system on a sound basis. They will minimize selfish group action, looking simply to an increase in benefits. They will bring to the employee the feeling of self-respect and self-assurance that come from thrift and savings, and making provision for one's own future.

It goes without saying that under this system the employee or his heirs should be entitled to his contributions, with interest, upon termination of his employment for any reason whatsoever, and that, from an accounting standpoint, contributions of employers and employees should be kept separate.

The principle that the amount of benefit received by a given employee should bear a relation to the length of his employment, has been incorporated in practically all unemployment insurance programs.

The unemployment insurance program in Great Britain in the beginning provided that benefit was to be paid strictly according to the number of contributions made by and on behalf of the employee, and only for a limited period within each twelve months. As the unemployment insurance system was expanded, however, to include relief for the unemployed in the form of transitional benefits, this principle was gradually abandoned, until the point was reached where no trace remained either of the principle of direct ratio, or of yearly limit. The results were singularly unfortunate, and the original principle has now been restored. If a person has paid thirty contributions into the insurance fund during the last two years, he may, if out of work, draw twenty-six weeks of benefit. If he has been in assurance for five years, he may draw an additional twenty-six weeks of benefit. For longer periods of assurance, there is a somewhat longer allowance of benefit. Where a person runs out of benefit, and is still unemployed, his case now has to be taken up by the Public Assistance Authority.

In this country, the Wisconsin law provides that, within definite limits, the payments of benefits are to be in proportion to the length of employment during the preceding year. The Ohio bill provides that no employee shall be entitled to any benefits unless he or she has been employed and has paid premiums for not less than twenty-six weeks within the twelve months preceding the date of the application for benefits, or unless he or she has been so employed and paid such premiums for a period of forty weeks during the two years preceding the date of application.

There seems to be no doubt as to the soundness of the principle, or as to the advisability of incorporating it into any system that may be set up.

And this is likewise true as to the provision for a waiting period prior to the actual beginning of benefit payments.

Finally, we come to the question as to who shall be charged with the responsibility of investing the reserve funds. This is most decidedly a State function. The principal fiscal officer of the State should be charged with the responsibility. He should be limited to investments in State Bonds. He should likewise be held responsible for setting up an adequate system of distribution.

You will realize, of course, that in this brief outline I have done little more than sketch some of the principal questions which will inevitably arise in attempting to mitigate in part the hardships of unemployment by making provision in advance for the kind of unemployment which may be covered by a system of reserves. Let me again remind you that such a program must be kept entirely separate from the relief problem; that it will not take care of general unemployment over the entire period of a protracted depression; and, at best, it can serve only as a first line of defense. But, within the limits above outlined, it would, in my judgment, represent a genuine step forward toward that economic security to which people so justly aspire.

November, 1934.